A partnership between American Library Association
and FINRA Investor Education Foundation

FINRA is proud to support the American Library Association

PROFITING
IN
ECONOMIC
STORMS

PROFITING
IN
ECONOMIC
STORMS

A HISTORIC GUIDE TO

Surviving Depression, Deflation,
Hyperinflation, and Market Bubbles

DANIEL S. SHAFFER

WILEY

John Wiley & Sons, Inc.

Published by John Wiley & Sons, Inc., Hoboken, New Jersey.
Published simultaneously in Canada.

For general information on our other products and services or for technical support, please contact our Customer Care Department within the United States at (800) 762-2974, outside the United States at (317) 572-3993 or fax (317) 572-4002.

Wiley also publishes its books in a variety of electronic formats. Some content that appears in print may not be available in electronic books. For more information about Wiley products, visit our web site at www.wiley.com.

Library of Congress Cataloging-in-Publication Data:

Shaffer, Daniel S., 1961–
    Profiting in economic storms : a historic guide to surviving depression, deflation, hyperinflation, and market bubbles / Daniel S. Shaffer.
        p.   cm.
    Includes index.
    ISBN 978-0-470-59633-3 (cloth); ISBN 978-0-470-90658-3 (ebk);
    ISBN 978-0-470-90659-0 (ebk); ISBN 978-0-470-90660-6 (ebk)
        1. Financial crises.   2. Economic stabilization.   3. Deflation (Finance)
    4. Inflation (Finance)   I. Title.
    HB3722.S486   2011
    332.6—dc22

                                                                2010034715

Printed in the United States of America

10 9 8 7 6 5 4 3 2 1

To my three boys: Jared, Matthew, and Benjamin. You give me the capacity to keep learning as I follow along in my quest for knowledge and understanding.

Contents

Preface

After many years of speaking about valuable investment, trading, and money management methodologies that I've accumulated throughout my career, I decided to write this book to share my research and thoughts with the goal to help other investors, traders, and money managers achieve great success in the current and future economic storms.

I began my career on Wall Street literally from the pits. In January 1983, after I graduated early from Syracuse University in December 1982, I became a floor trader on the New York Futures Exchange trading the New York Composite Index futures contract right next door to the New York Stock Exchange. A month later, I was hired by Jimmy Cayne to join Bear Stearns & Company as a commodity broker. As a commodity futures trader back in those days, I recall trading the U.S. Treasury bond futures along with other commodity futures. We all used to huddle around the Reuters machine on the 49th floor of 55 Water Street in lower Manhattan late Thursday afternoons after the markets closed to see the weekly release of the money supply numbers. After the release, we would all watch the long bond

(30 year U.S. Treasury) cash market trade as futures back then had floor trading hours only and were closed. I was hooked.

After years of being involved in the business, I've come to find out that there are innumerable factors at work determining how the markets behave. It's not an easy study. I start this book by discussing the current economic storm and then move into Part One, a section focused on human nature.

In Part One, I describe how natural human instincts influence trading and the direction of the markets. We all need to recognize that some instincts can be destructive not only with our investment decisions but also with life decisions. Investing is not an easy game to play. For example, during the upward swings in bull market cycles, a trader can become convinced of his own genius because the tide takes most stocks higher. Greed causes us to pile onto an experience until it turns on us. The problem lies in the mere thought that the market will continue to go up forever and that it is still possible to make the easy money. During the bull market run in the 1990s, I met many people who quit their day jobs because they were making so much money in the market. The bust of the NASDAQ market certainly put many of those investors back in the work force as the trend change caught most by surprise. We can see this in the reduced volume levels of the stock markets over the years.

I also describe in Part One that we are a reflection of what we want to get out of the market or our investments. Some people are thrill seekers and enjoy the excitement of the markets without a goal of making money or controlling risk. Others are able to tame the emotions within themselves and become tremendous successes as they choose to be winners and have a positive mental attitude toward winning. They realize that losing is part of the game and accept small losses in order to build a long-lasting relationship with the markets.

In Part Two, I aim to show the reality of the numbers and methods that make and influence our financial system. The markets do not act accordingly to the information because of the inconsistency of the accuracy in the data. The truth may never be told but the reactions of the markets are real. One thought that I hear many times over is that no matter what you believe or what the data appear to be saying, the markets are always right. It's just a matter of being one with the market. With individual stocks, I review how income statements and balance sheets can be misleading and you must read between the lines very carefully to determine the truth behind the numbers. It could save you from an Enron-type fraud or similar financial disaster.

At the end of Part Two, I discuss the concept of modern port-folio theory and asset allocation. In certain time periods the theory seems to have worked—such as the period between 1982 and 2006. But because the theory is connected to the efficient frontier and the efficient market hypothesis, the theory was quickly disproven as the markets tumbled lower as almost every sector and asset class found heavy liquidation in a panic-selling environment. If the markets were efficient and all the available information was priced into the markets and human emotions were not part of the equation, then there would be a chance that modern portfolio theory could work. But, in my opinion, such is not the case and the recent market volatility and sharp movements lower of panic selling dispelled that the markets were anywhere near efficient. Beware of those hawking asset allo-cation based on previous historical models because of their inherent flaws of not identifying periods in which those models did not work.

Part Three is a history lesson of sorts. The history of the U.S. banking system goes quite a lot deeper than I was able to present. In fact, I probably could have written a whole book on this subject, but I wanted to give you the highlights and turning points that make up the current banking system. It is an ever-evolving machine that will have no end point but I do suspect that the current system which is now under fire by some very smart representatives in House and Senate is only at the early stages of change. Remember, the current Federal Reserve was created in 1913 because of an event in the early 1900s that was the catalyst for change. I believe that we are on the cusp of another major catalyst in the next few years that will again change the structure of the current banking system as we know it today. Be on the lookout for such a catalyst, which I suspect will be the decline of equity markets to such extreme low levels that the people of the United States will demand something be done to fix the system. The answer is yet to be discovered.

Also in Part Three, I present the history of three fallen civilizations, the Roman Empire, classical Greece, and ancient Egypt. All of these civilizations had a common thread, which led to their demise. The level of comfort of the leaders or the elite who thought that their power would go on forever was the thinking that brought them down in the end. Today, here in the United States, many of us believe that we are the superpower. I would not disagree, but as history shows us, nothing lasts forever. The United States is, and I say this with respect, only 234 years old. The Declaration of Independence was our break from British rule. We are a young county compared to the thousands of years of the history of other civilizations. Throughout history, power moves from country to country depending on the political and monetary powers. The United States with all of its debt is at a weak point financially which could cause us to lose our elite status in world politics. On the other hand, China is currently one of the fastest growing countries in a monetary sense as they have a surplus of funds and are coming into the modern age by building up their infrastructure. We should all be aware that change is in the air and invest accordingly. The Chinese markets, though, may be in a mania phase similar to the famous market manias presented in the last chapter of Part Three. Manias can be very magnetic and convince one that trees grow to the sky. As I describe throughout this book, cycles are everywhere and we need to recognize them the best we can based on the information available. In 1990, the Japanese markets were in a mania that brought them down approximately 75 percent from their peak. And don't forget the mania of the dot.com era with the NASDAQ market. Manias have existed throughout history and will continue as long as the element of emotion is involved in the markets. The Chinese market may be the next mania; Time will tell.

In Part Four, I present natural occurrences that can be tied into the market cycles. The relationship between the earth, moon, and sun has been studied by many and I believe has validity as to correlation with many different market movements, most of all the stock market. Sunspot cycles, climate change, and the natural law of the universe for environmental cycles can be very powerful in predicting and analyzing movements in the longer term cycles of the stock market. Further studies such as the Elliott Wave Theory and Fibonacci sequences give a real mathematical understanding of the order of the universe, and transposing those methods to the stock market movements can be a real eye opener. The T Theory concept uses imagery to locate cycle beginnings and ends in all different time frames that can assist you in the methods of entry and exit rules.

Finally, in Part Four, I discuss that markets *are* engineered. Throughout this book, I discuss longer term cycles such as years, months, and weeks, but even every day, there are market movement observations that can sometimes be explained in mathematical terms. I have presented formulas commonly used by traders and shared some observations of a champion trader who was kind enough to share them with me.

You must understand the game in order to make money during different market cycles. Control your losses so you can come back and invest with more confidence.

Acknowledgments

I would like to thank my parents for giving me the ability to think
critically and develop my own point of view, for the uncondi-
tional love they constantly gave to me and my brothers, and for
making sacrifices so that I could have the education I received.

Thanks to J. Welles Wilder Jr. and the staff of the Delta Society
International, Robert Prechter Jr. and the staff of Elliott Wave International, Terrence Laundry and the staff of the T Theory Foundation,
and Martin "Buzzy" Schwartz—a champion trader—for allowing
me to share their research and studies.

To the staff at Morningstar, Inc., Genesis Financial Technologies,
Inc., and TradeStation Group, Inc., for allowing me to use their data
and software graphics.

To all the people at John Wiley & Sons who helped make this
book a reality. Special thanks to Kevin Commins and Meg Freeborn
for not only their great editorial assistance but for their encouragement, guidance, and patience toward me as a first time author.

And thanks to Thomas J. Berthel, who continues to inspire and
encourage others to be the best that they can be, especially during
economic storms.

PROFITING
IN
ECONOMIC
STORMS

Chapter 1

The Current Economic Storm

I t has been said that when your neighbor is out of a job it's a recession. But when you are out of a job, it's a depression. In the United States, the mood of individuals in this current economic environment has surely changed. Unemployment is rising, spending is declining, and asset values have burst from a seemingly high level. But this mood may not only be isolated in the United States, as many other countries around the world are struggling with their own sovereign debt and internal financial issues as the current storm spreads globally.

If the economy is doing as well as portrayed in the media then why are housing prices continuing to decline and the price of goods falling? My answer is simple. Don't believe everything you hear or read. The real truth about the economy is reflected in your budget and spending habits.

Is It Deflation or Depression?

Deflation is when aggregate demand is less than supply of goods and services, thus general price levels drop. It's not that we don't have a surplus of goods and services; rather, we are experiencing a collapse of aggregate demand. We are entering a new but old economic era where the U.S. economy has been before. We are not only experiencing another major decline in the stock market similar to the Great Depression, but we are also reliving the large amounts of fraud embedded in our financial environment that accompanied that time period. In my opinion, contrary to what our leaders are boasting, it is not over yet and we are in the early stages of a Great Deflationary Depression. This just may be the beginning of a multi-year period of slow or negative economic growth not seen since the Great Depression.

A depression is a sustained, long downturn in an economy or a long-lasting recession. Recessions can be considered healthy for an economy. For instance, if growth starts to accelerate and signs of inflation seep into an economy as seen by too much demand for the amount of goods or services available, then a cooling-off period may materialize to slow down the demand and keep prices within a reasonable growth rate. The U.S. Federal Reserve has power to raise interest rates, which slows down the economy by increasing the cost of borrowing money, thus taking dollars out of the money supply as a goal of slowing demand. The opposite is true of a recession. The Federal Reserve will lower interest rates in an attempt to inflate the economy, thereby decreasing the cost of borrowing money and increasing the amount of money supply as a goal of inflating the economy.

Unfortunately, this is not an exact science and the Federal Reserve can get it wrong. Between 2001 and 2006, the Federal Reserve had a policy to keep money flowing, which caused a huge bubble in real estate and financial paper assets. In its final stage in 2008, commodity prices rallied to extreme levels in a parabolic manner that eventually had to crash. By the end of 2008, most asset classes crashed at the same time. Equities, real estate, oil, grains, metals (precious and non-precious) and basic material prices fell in tandem with each other as the over-leverage in the financial system began to fall apart.

As the cost of money was so low, speculators borrowed as much as the system would allow and purchased as many assets as they could get their hands on. Speculators are investors such as individuals, hedge funds, pension plans and other similar entities that attempt to profit on price movements as markets rise and fall. A major problem inherent within the financial system was that speculators were able to purchase most asset classes with minimal actual investment dollars as leverage was the name of the game. A speculator could buy a house with little money down or buy futures contracts on crude oil for speculation with approximately five percent down. The problem was that if and when prices declined, the speculators would have to put up more money or sell out the asset to cut their losses. In reality, as prices collapsed, the global speculators had one huge margin call.

To meet the margin call, speculators turned to their usual resources: banks. Unfortunately, bankers had also become speculators along with nonbank speculators for the opportunity to enhance returns to compete with the nonbank investment firms. This created a domino reaction that started as the first speculator couldn't meet his or her margin call. The massive selling of the underlying assets encouraged other margin call speculators to unload their assets after realizing what was happening. The global assets started to implode and prices started to drop at an accelerated rate.

Now, realize that it took from 1983 to 2007 to create this massive bubble of asset appreciation. History has shown that a multi-decade bubble of such magnitude does not clean itself out in two years. I believe that it will take at least half the time of the building of the bubble to correct itself before prices of goods and services can be realigned for the next growth cycle. Therefore, I believe the next growth cycle will begin in 2020. Until then, our economy will experience a multiyear deflationary cycle that could see assets fall as far as 90 percent from their peaks in 2007–2008. Do you find that hard to believe? Well, in the Roaring Twenties, most believed that such a fall could not happen, but it did. In my opinion, a depression started in 2008 and we are only two years into my expected cycle of 12 years.

As deflation begins, the buying power of your dollar in the United States will get stronger regardless of the value of the dollar versus other world currencies. You will be able to buy more goods and services as deflation cuts prices to stimulate movement. You want to be in a position to take advantage of the low-priced asset environment to come.

Currently, I hear advisors hawking gold and other hard assets. I believe that this couldn't be farther from the truth. These people have been trained to believe that as the Federal Reserve keeps pumping money into the financial system, it will cause an inflationary environment. Based on my calculations, the amount of money being pumped into the U.S. financial system is still less than the value of the assets that were highly leveraged—whose values have been destroyed by the bubble bursting in such assets as real estate and the stock market values up to now. But on top of this, our leaders are actually prolonging the length and deepness of the depression. They are preaching that in order to get out of the deepest recession since the Great Depression, we must go further into debt. How can the debt problem that was caused by a spending free-for-all be corrected if people are being told that going into more debt will solve the problem? This is absurd and will never work. Japan tried this method and it got them to the same place we are headed for here in the United States, a prolonged deep recession that I describe as a deflationary depression.

The Government Cannot Save this Sinking Ship

History has shown that when governments get involved with capitalistic societies, the rules begin to change. For example in 1920, the U.S.

economy was about to go into a deep recession. The government at that time had the ability to choose to intervene or let the natural order of capitalism take place. The choice was made not to interfere with capitalism and as companies failed, the economy began to flourish. The result of the no-action policy was rewarded with healthy economic growth all during the Roaring Twenties until the crash of 1929.

After the crash of 1929, which was caused by too much speculation, the government decided that it needed to do something drastic to start policies that they believed would get the economy back on track. However, government intervention had the opposite effect. Programs were designed to encourage people to rely on the government instead of on themselves. Many were looking for handouts, as we may be experiencing today.

At the same time, the agricultural economy was starting to deteriorate as climate change reduced crop production during the dust bowl period which resulted in more people out of work.

Finally, during the 1930s, the newly born Federal Reserve developed policies that were more restrictive than expansive due to lack of experience by the Fed officials as to how to handle the economic environment. A restrictive policy resulted in a continuation of the depression which ended up being one of the worst economic depressions known as the Great Depression.

As for today, I see history repeating itself. Starting in 2004 through the peak in 2007, the real estate housing market began to teeter after a wild increase of housing prices for many years. The later years were the most exciting as housing prices ran up into 2006. However, warning signs were beginning to show up in the cracks and the government, instead of allowing prices to moderate, developed plans to get almost everyone into the housing game. We recently found out through congressional hearings that banks and other financial institutions were encouraged to continue lending money to people that would have never qualified for mortgages, just to keep the game going. On top of that program, Wall Street firms were packaging these low-quality loans as investments to pension funds and individual investors alike, not only here but also abroad.

Inevitably by late 2007, the bottom was beginning to fall out and housing prices began to collapse as mortgage defaults and sales began hitting the markets at a rate faster than the markets could absorb. At first, our leaders said that the housing financial problem would be contained and would not spread to the rest of the economy. Unfortunately, in my opinion and that of others I clearly respect, the housing market is the backbone of any economy. Housing supports many professions and manufacturing companies and without a strong housing market, these industries will begin to feel the effects, resulting in layoffs and increased unemployment.

The cycle then begins. Housing starts and sales of existing homes begin to fall. Then, mortgage defaults start to rise, putting more houses on the market competing with new homes that were being built at a rapid speculative rate. Continuing along this cycle, as the values of the homes that were financed to the maximum levels fall below their respective mortgage balances, homeowners start walking away from their homes, thereby leaving the value of their neighbors' homes to decline. The final result ends up being high unemployment.

The Federal Reserve then steps in and drops interest rates to practically zero for banks to borrow so that they can lend to prospective homebuyers. But this is the part of the equation that no one, in my opinion, expected: The demand for mortgages and loans dropped to extremely low levels. The psychology of the consumer began to change. People stopped buying homes and even started to slow down buying durable goods on credit. The loans on the books of many banks and financial institutions began to crumble. The Federal Reserve had already dropped interest rates to historically low levels, so the next plan was for the Federal Reserve to buy up the nonperforming loans from the banks and financial institutions in hope of flooding the markets with capital. Unfortunately, this program didn't seem to help create demand. In fact, many economists and economic advisors thought it would be inflationary.

My opinion is that the Federal Reserve could not replace enough lost money back into the system. All they did was remove toxic nonperforming assets from the banks and financial institutions and put them on the Federal Reserve balance sheet. Future generations will most likely foot the bill for this program.

I conclude that the government cannot stimulate demand for credit in a deflating, over-leveraged society. They cannot change the attitude that took an about-face when it went from "I want it now" to "I need to conserve" thinking. Credit demand will continue to slow for years to come as households, small businesses, and even major publicly traded corporations realign their balance sheets and hoard cash. These are truly signs of a deflationary depression.

Protecting What You Have

Batten down the hatches and preserve your money now. If you own fully invested stock market vehicles such as mutual funds, you might want to think about getting out now. In my opinion, if you have excess money in bank accounts above Federal Deposit Insurance Corporation (FDIC) protection levels, invest that money in short-term U.S. Treasuries in such time periods as 3-month Treasury bills to 2-year Treasury notes. Be aware that it is not the time to think about or hope for return on your money. You should be concerned about the return of your money when you will need it the most. Even if the banking system defaults, you can still go to the U.S. Treasury and redeem your bills, notes, and bonds. Back in the earlier stages of the Great Depression, there were such days as a bank holiday. These bank holidays were designed to cool the public down from panic about getting access to their money.

Today, we have the FDIC, which is an agency of the U.S. Government designed to guarantee deposits up to certain amounts per account per customer at its member banks. The guarantee fund used by the FDIC gets its fund from assessments from the very banks it protects. Unfortunately, that fund ran out of money and assessed the banks in 2010 for years to come just to put money back in the FDIC pot. The funds are again running out of money due to the continual failures of banks. The FDIC's own reports indicate that they expect over 400 banks to fail by 2012. Furthermore, there is an available credit line from the U.S. Treasury to the FDIC, but if tapped into then the U.S. Treasury would have to issue more bonds (debt), because by my calculations, they don't have the resources on hand to cover the credit line as tax receipts have been declining and government policies have been spending.

Today, our government is financing its operations by issuing U.S. government securities such as Treasury bills, notes, and bonds. But buyers of large amounts of these U.S. Treasuries are foreign central banks such as China and our own Federal Reserve! Sounds like a Ponzi scheme to me. The U.S. Treasury is issuing securities and our Federal Reserve is buying them. Not only is the Federal Reserve buying the debt that the United States is issuing, but they are also buying toxic debt from the banks to put cash in the banking system. I will go into more detail about this later in this book, but be aware that I question the validity of the Federal Reserve as an agency of the U.S. Government as it is stated in their own brochure; in my opinion, it seems that it stands on its own as a separate entity.

Deflation is here and getting worse. Keep liquid and safe with your money and preserve it for future financial purchases at lower prices over the coming depression. You may see bargains that you can only imagine right now.

Profiting from the Coming Deflationary Depression

There are several ways to profit in a recession. The first way is to realize that cash is king. Bargains will appear whether in goods at stores dropping in price so inventory can move, or real asset prices such as real estate, precious metals, and other tangible assets as investments get liquidated at obscene prices. Services such as home repair, auto repair, and personal care, among others, may see their prices drop. So being patient as the deflation cycle develops will give you tremendous opportunity to take advantage of a lower cost environment.

I also believe that the equity markets will also deflate with the deflation cycle. Investors will not only liquidate to raise capital, but the future company earnings, which stock prices are supposed to reflect, may decline to lower levels, thereby dragging down stock prices.

In the 1929 stock market crash and subsequent years as the markets moved lower, there were aggressive investors who sold stocks short. Shorting stocks means that you borrow the stock from another investor and sell it to a buyer. Your bet is that the stock will move lower and you will be able to buy it back in the future at the lower price and redeliver it to the investor you borrowed it from. This is one way of profiting in a potential declining market.

Fortunately, today's investors can choose from derivatives such as options, futures, and exchange traded funds (ETFs) to profit in a declining stock market. If you choose options, put buying would be the position of profiting as the market moves lower. The only problem is that if the market doesn't move lower then you will lose money on that bet. The fortunate part is that with put buying, you can only lose as much as you invested. It's a bit more complicated than what I have explained here and I do recommend that you seek out professional help before taking any of this advice.

Also, as a derivative, one can sell a stock index futures contract to buy back at a later date. There are futures contracts on the major stock market indexes such as the Dow Jones Industrial Average, the S&P 500, the NASDAQ, and the Russell 2000 indexes. Again, I caution you that these vehicles are risky and you should consult a professional advisor if you choose to use these vehicles to make a bet on the future of the market.

Finally, there are ETFs that you can buy like a stock where the value has the potential to increase as the markets decline. These vehicles are getting more popular especially because of their liquidity and ease of trading. Another plus is that ETFs can be used as vehicles in an IRA account or other similar plans that have restrictions on the availability to invest in other derivatives such as options and futures.

Somewhere in this cycle will be a great opportunity to purchase stock of major corporations at rock-bottom prices. The Great Depression–type levels or the levels of the Japanese stock prices that declined for the past decade will be seen here in the U.S. markets in the future. Throughout this book, you will read about points and time levels where great opportunities may show themselves for entry into the equity markets, but for now think in terms of deflation. This means lower prices ahead for mostly every sector of the economy as liquidation continues to take place until we run out of sellers.

Preparing for the Next Hyperinflation Cycle

Eventually, once the deflationary depression cycle runs its course, we will need to prepare to invest in the coming hyperinflationary cycle. I do warn that this cycle is many years away as the current deflationary cycle needs to bottom first. Of course, when we reach that bottom, the government and the economic advisors may not see it and keep policies of money expansion on too long.

If the money expansion policies are not curtailed in time then the probability of the hyperinflation exists. We anticipate that hyperinflation will be the result of loose government policies held too long, and our current target for the peak in hyperinflation is around the year 2020. In later chapters in the book, we will note our expected target for the peak in gold, which is known as a safe haven for hyperinflationary parts of the economic cycle.

Summary

Almost every major depression in the history of the United States has been greeted with a substantial decline in the money supply.

This decline is also often accompanied by a collapse of the banking system in some shape or form. During major depressions, money and banking center difficulties are among the major causes of the declining economic climate.

For thousands of years through the ups and downs of economic cycles, people have always had trouble with money. They complain about inflation and blame it on an excess increase in the money supply. Or, they have trouble in recessions with unemployment moving higher, factories sitting idle, and falling prices of consumer goods and services and then complain that the money supply is declining and not growing rapidly enough. The point is that there is seldom that exact point where demand equals supply, as we learn in Economics 101, where there is in theory just the right amount of money in circulation. A multitude of policies have been tested and tried to control the money supply for hundreds of years, yet none have gotten it exactly correct.

Throughout the history of expansion and contraction of our economy, it is clear that money is the most important element to all of us. Our current system, after centuries of experiments, has created sophisticated measures to control the money supply in the interest of the public. But, through it all, this only raises new questions about how these new measures of power should be used.

Consumer and corporate expenditures for goods and services, particularly investment expenditures, are greatly influenced by the money supply. The management of the money supply affects four of the major objectives of economic policy: full employment, price stability, growth, and balance of payments equilibrium, which is very difficult to get exactly right.

As the goal of the current Federal Reserve System is to influence expenditures for goods and services through its control over the money supply, its policies cause economic depressions, deflation, hyperinflation, and market bubbles, although indirectly. Such changes in the money supply also influence the behavior of banks and other lending agencies where they may take on too much risk or curtail risk when the environment is uncertain. As a result of all of these variables, changes in interest rates and the availability of credit strongly influence expenditures for business investment, construction of houses, and other types of spending. But the underlying measure is the psychology of the consuming public. If they become scared and stop spending, as we are beginning to experience in this current cycle, then no policy of the Federal Reserve or U.S. government or bank lending capability will stop a deflationary cycle.

Part One

HUMAN NATURE IN ECONOMIC STORMS

Chapter 2

Battling Your
Natural Instincts

A s human beings, we have been given the ability to think, rationalize, and reason in ways the animal kingdom cannot. Unfortunately, most of us don't take advantage of these gifts. Animals rely on their instincts to survive every day; they wake up, follow their instincts, and then do it again the next day. Their battle is for food, shelter, and protection from predators. They are born with completely natural instincts and each species has its own set of predetermined lifestyles that they practice during their lifetime.

As we travel through life there are decisions that need to be made. Sometimes we rely on our natural instincts to resolve or improve a situation only to find out afterward that if we had chosen to rationalize and reason through the situation, it may have turned out more effectively. Having the ability to step back from the big picture and look at the strokes on the canvas can give you a better understanding of your standing and improve your decision-making process. Those strokes are the makeup of your future.

Some decisions are forced upon us through nature and some are the result of circumstances that we have created. For instance, my first son, Jared, was born with severe mental disabilities, a situation that was forced upon me by nature and changed my life forever. And for readers that have had similar experiences, my heart goes out to you for your courage and devotion. At the moment of discovery, my emotions ran through my body to my brain in a way that I had never felt before. I had no choice but to evaluate the situation and circumstances before me. I realized life had just taken a turn down the road less traveled by many but it was those who did travel that road that I needed to search out for strength. We can learn a great deal from others.

On the other hand, in our journeys through life, circumstances become available or doors open that can give us great opportunities to grow, prosper, and enjoy life, if we make sensible choices. For instance, I have been faced with many career choices. My choice was to do what I enjoyed. Through conversations with people, I find that most don't enjoy what they do. Then why do it? Because I find joy in what I do, it's easy for me to get out of bed in the morning but I find it much harder to shut down to go to sleep at night. I enjoy what I do because the career I have chosen is to learn and never stop learning. This philosophy keeps me young and active.

The Hopeful Investor

Nature allows us to have two very important elements: hope and fear. As human beings, we can be very hopeful through difficult situations or decisions. In determining an investment strategy, that hopefulness can be a danger.

For instance, if a broker calls you and pitches a particular stock to buy, you are hopeful that it will be a good choice. Let's use an example of a stock at a price of $50. You now own, based on a recommendation by your broker or from your own choosing, a stock at $50. Within a period of time the stock moves lower to $40. What is the most common response from your broker or from your own mind? "Well, I liked it at $50 so I must love it at $40." Most people will begin the natural thought process of holding on to the stock for two reasons: (1) "I can't be wrong," or (2) "I am hopeful that the stock will move back higher and I will break even." (I note here that the market does not know or care where you bought the stock.) Many even go as far as to buy more of the same losing stock. There is a rule that I always remember: Don't add to a losing position. But, unfortunately, nature keeps us believing that the final outcome will be in our favor. In our example, the investor ends up holding the stock or buying more of the same stock to prove to his ego that he can't be wrong.

Now, let's take this example to the next level. The investor made an original purchase of a stock at $50, the stock price declined to $40, and the example investor purchased more of the same stock. Now, several weeks later, the stock is at $30. What does the example investor do now? Well, the ego and hopefulness lingers in his brains and nature tells him to hold on and see what happens. So, the example investor watches the stock move from $30 to $20 or even lower. When does he get out? Usually an investor starts to feel the pain and decides to get out near the lows because the mental and physical pain is too much to bear. The loss is taken, the ego is bruised and the hopefulness has disappeared.

The above example has occurred time and time again throughout investing history. It has happened ever since stock pricing was created. Now, let's turn back to our example investor who not only lost money on a single stock, but has done this time after time after time. In other words, the negative outcome experience is embedded in his brain as nature makes it a permanent experience to be remembered, which can affect the outcome of a potentially positive experience as I discuss in the next section.

The Fearful Investor

Now, let me introduce the fear side of hope and fear emotions. Let's now say the example investor purchases a stock either on the recommendation of his broker, or on his own accord. The stock price is $50. Now, several weeks later, the example investor checks the stock price and it has reached $60. The example investor now thinks he has profited and his ego is fulfilled. Now the investor needs to make a decision. What does the example investor do? The first thought that goes through his mind is that he was right and made a good investment. He feels good about himself and feels a little proud. But, the next move is the most common: Thinking about all his past losses that have been embedded in his brain to remember, he sells the stock for fear of losing a profit. At that moment, the investor feels euphoric, thinking he finally got it right. He has bought a stock and sold it for a profit.

But, did he really get it right? After the example investor sells his stock, the price begins to rise further. Remember, the example investor bought the stock at $50, sold it at $60, and now the stock is at $70. Not only that, but the stock continues to climb to $80 or higher. What actually transpired was that the example investor was so accustomed to taking losses that when he finally had a winner, the fear of losing a profit took over his thought process. He had a high probability winning trade. As the price was moving up, he could have had a highly probable chance of profiting by purchasing more of it, instead of selling the stock.

The opportunity, in our example for the hopeful investor, would have been to sell the losing trade or stock if it failed to follow through and not to add to the losing position on hope that it would rebound. And, the opportunity on the winning trade would have been to buy more of the stock as it was trending up, as it had moved according to expectations of making money. In summary, one cannot have a long-term positive result by taking large losses and small profits.

We must retrain our brains to combat some of the instincts that nature gave us. Instead of hope that our losses recover to break even or become profitable and fear of giving back profits in a winning position only to find that the profits could have been greater, we must retrain or reverse our brains to the thought process of hoping our profits continue to rise and fearing losses. The long-term goal is never to take a large loss. We can take many small losses and many small gains for the eventuality of having a larger profit from time to time, but the most important concept is to avoid the large losing trades. Take a moment to think in terms of probabilities: If you exclude large losses from your trading, and you have small losses and small gains, then eventually the large gains will surprise you and add to your investment portfolio with controlled risk.

In our thinking processes we also need to be aware of the critical input that we receive from others. Whether it's input from a spouse, friend, associate, or other influential person in your life, always remember that your decisions from the hope versus fear process will ultimately affect you mentally and your future potential, not them. When asking for input from others, consider their motives and beware of unsolicited advice. Personally, I don't give unsolicited advice, and when asked, I always proclaim that it is only my opinion. People like to do what I refer to as herd or crowd behavior; they want to do what other people are doing because it makes them more comfortable. It's difficult to go against the crowd but that is where some of the big money is made.

The Herd or Crowd Effect

Similar to animals acting the same in a herd moving in one direction, when individuals become crowds they tend to also follow what the group is doing, which is the most comfortable decision to make. As the markets cycle from boom to bust and back again we must remember who we are and what perspective we are coming from. Right now we are on the other side of the boom cycle. The markets have had an outstanding money-making opportunity since August of 1982 with a few bumps along the way.

The herd or crowd effect has a tremendous influence on our investment philosophy. During the 1990s, the crowd was excited about all the great buying opportunities and expressing strongly that the stock markets were poised to grow to the sky, reaching excessive new highs. The roaring bull market was a money-making machine. This cycle through the 1990s had most investors convinced that stock markets don't cycle down; they reasoned that problems associated with historical declines had been solved and were a thing of the past. Individual investors believed they knew how the game worked so they ignored the advice of brokers and advisors and continued opening self-managed discount accounts.

Then dot.com stocks arrived. These were companies with great concepts that were perceived to make zillions of profits by use of the Internet. Investors were stepping over each other to grab not only the existing stocks in this particular universe, but as new stocks were being issued, the prices on the first day of trading went out of sight. The crowd was gathering for the most exciting prospect of gaining wealth since the concept of the gold rush. Most of these companies were still in the development stage and some were even losing money. But, everyone was talking about this new phenomenon, companies that can make money over the Internet.

Most of these stocks were listed on the NASDAQ exchange. The NASDAQ exchange is an over-the-counter electronic exchange unlike the New York Stock Exchange or the American Stock Exchange, which at the time were floor-traded exchanges with real bodies in front of a booth where a company's stock would trade. The advantage of the floor trading exchange was having a specialist behind the trading of a particular stock whose job it was to keep the stock trading in an orderly fashion. But, on the NASDAQ exchange, orders were executed on a computer system where it was difficult to get a feel for the activity of a particular stock.

Nevertheless, leading up to the year 2000, the NASDAQ index soared to a parabolic height. On December 31, 1990, the NASDAQ

Composite Index closed at 373.80. As the crowd started to gather momentum and the Internet became the next frontier, an interim low was put in by a minor broad market sell-off triggered by the troubles of Long-Term Capital Management back on October 8, 1998, at 1,343.47. At this point in time, the shoeshine boys, cab drivers, and everyone I spoke to at cocktail parties were discussing the hot stocks to buy on the NASDAQ before this index took its final parabolic push higher. By this point, the index was up already over 259 percent. As the crowd continued its belief that money could be made and that any company that ended in or had the term dot.com associated with it was a sure winner, the index continued its unprecedented climb and on March 10, 2000, as shown graphically in Figure 2.1 the NASDAQ index reached an interim day high of 5,132.52! This was a total return

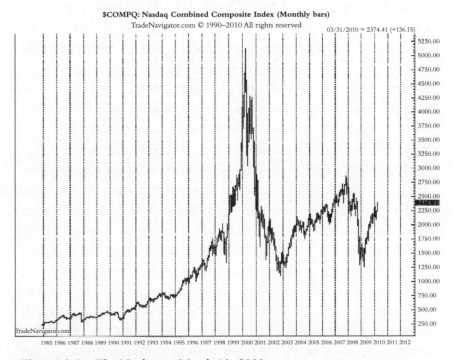

Figure 2.1 The Nasdaq on March 10, 2000

SOURCE: Prepared by Shaffer Asset Management, Inc. Copyrighted 2009 by Genesis Financial Technologies, Inc.

of 1,273 percent from December 31, 1990, and a total return of 282 percent from October 8, 1998.

The returns were so exciting to many that it reminded me of the Roaring Twenties and we all know how that ended. Investors' excitement didn't falter when the cycle ended: They continued to pile in even as the market was coming down. They were trained as a crowd by the long period of the 1990s that this was the way to financial freedom. Many people with full-time jobs were day- or swing trading stocks from their computer terminals and some were making so much money that they quit their day jobs and began day trading from home. The concept was to buy in the morning and sell in the afternoon and go out and celebrate that evening. Restaurants were definitely reaping the boom benefits.

Well, the bull market in the NASDAQ ended in 2000 and it has been in a bear market ever since. The fact is that by October 10, 2002, the NASDAQ Composite Index reached a low of 1,108.49, a 78 percent decline since its peak. The low in 2002 reached as far down as the levels way back in 1996, some six years earlier.

This was another lesson in history of how the crowd effect can make or break a fortune. I have heard many stories of fortunes wiped out because of the belief that the stocks would come back.

The NASDAQ Composite Index made a slight comeback to 2,861.51 over the years as the Dow Jones Industrial Average and the S&P 500, among other indexes, reached their peaks in October 2007. Since then, the NASDAQ Composite took another tumble into the recent lows of March of 2009 to a low of 1,265.62. Again, a 55.77 percent loss from its 2007 peak.

I emphasize the NASDAQ Composite cycle peak and decline as a current cycle today because it has been the most recent experienced and should be fresh in our minds. Today, we are experiencing similar patterns in the Dow Jones Industrial Average and the S&P 500 Index as compared to the NASDAQ, separated by seven years. The crowd lifted these indexes to all-time highs in 2007, then they fell dramatically in 2009, similar to the NASDAQ Composite, and now we are in the bounce phase of the longer term cycle which I believe will end pretty ugly. At this time, the crowd is following the advice of some economists and advisors who believe that the bottom of this cycle was in March 2009, which I believe was a short but strong bear market rally. This is just one of many examples throughout history of the crowd or herd effect moving prices of stocks or other goods such as the famous Gouda Tulip Bulb Mania of 1634–1637, which I will discuss in Chapter 7.

Believing in Others

Since it is our nature to question our own decisions, people tend to listen to what others say especially when their own decisions don't work out as expected. This does not mean that others have the answers but it seems that we seek out those who do. Our perception is to believe what others are saying so that we are either not alone in our thinking process or we confirm what we are already thinking.

If Thomas Edison or the Wright brothers had believed what others were telling them, then you may not have the great technology that you use today. This includes light bulbs, record players, telephones, and traveling from New York to California in six hours.

Another great example would be athletes who were told never to play their particular sport. If they had believed what was being told them, they would never have achieved such high levels of success.

Unfortunately, as humans, our sense of security relies on what other people say or think about us. When I speak out in the media, I am only giving my perspective of the way I see things. I am not telling investors what to do, I'm only giving guidance based on my beliefs and I expect them to interpret my thoughts into their own analysis. I will not always be correct in my analysis but the evidence that I use to come to my conclusions may be worth more than what I say.

We are not perfect as human beings but we share our search for the Holy Grail. We find gossip or rumors to be very exciting and influential, even when we do not know the sources or the facts. Same with investing, rumors and hot stock tips run rampant when it comes to making a quick buck or having an opportunity to get ahead of the crowd. So many of the rumors never pan out; they are just hype.

Rumors can be contagious and some start spreading them just to enhance the excitement in their lives or to increase others' interest to drive up the price of something they actually own. In the investment world this is called talking up your book, where book refers to one's holdings.

But, an important point to be made here is to consider the source. For instance, it would be very rare to hear an analyst or economist from a firm that seeks out investors to buy stocks, or for that matter other types of investments, to be negative on the overall stock market. That would be a self-defeating act and I would think that person's days would be numbered as an employee of such a firm. During the peak in the stock market in 2000 and the recent peak in 2007, how many analysts or economists employed by firms that want to keep investors in the markets discussed or signaled that the markets may be nearing a top? Furthermore, how many of these same people warned the investing public that as the market was declining, it may continue to decline for an extended period of time? I suspect very few, if any, were able to have the conviction to tell their clients or the firm's clients that a downward trend had a high probability of continuing. Even today, as I write this page, we are seeing an extreme bullishness in the indicators similar to the same areas that presented themselves as sell signals in 2007. But, in the media, the firms' analysts and economists, instead of stating that the market has gone too far and too fast, are touting that the stock market will continue to move higher and that one should be invested. Some have even raised their original targets since their first targets had already been met, but they should be saying that because their targets have been met, investors should now start lightening up on their exposure to the stock market.

Another group that you should be aware of are what I call the "cheerleaders." These are the employees, from the top all the way to the bottom, of a particular company that would never say anything negative about the prospects of the company they work for. It would be psychologically difficult for an employee to say anything negative about the company that employs them. Not only would it be emotionally difficult to themselves but would make them look socially weak in the eyes of the recipients of such information. I would never trust remarks from an employee of a company that I would consider investing in.

Summary

Taking stock in ourselves is just as important as investing in the markets. Through conscious awareness of our natural tendencies, we all have the ability to alter our thoughts to strive for positive results. The concept of hope and fear is one of the greatest topics I not only discuss in this book, but I also present in great detail in my speaking engagements. Furthermore, hope and fear are not only limited to investing, as these concepts may also be affecting your personal life. I recommend that you find your way around the herd or crowd effect because as an individual, you have the ability to think for yourself. When you are put in a situation of influence in a large group, you tend to question the validity of your own thoughts. Remember, some of the most productive inventions, creations, feats, and artwork are the results of one's own belief in himself or herself. Take heed where an opinion is coming from, as there may be an ulterior motive that you just may not see. Trust your instincts, cut your losses, and reevaluate the situation with a clear head and conscience. As you take a step back from the situation and review your results, you may see things more clearly. Finally, remember that cutting losses, letting profits grow, reaching targets, and keeping your ego out of the market are key factors to long-term success in your investment future.

Chapter 3

Getting What You Want Out of Life and Investing

During our life cycle, we all possess a unique psychological view. This is where our confidence, beliefs, self-esteem, and state of mind exist. We relate these traits to our everyday life decisions.

Determining what we want out of life comes from our desires for happiness and resolution. We cycle up and down during our lifetimes to achieve equilibrium in the phases that deeply affect us as human beings. Our internal cycles are greatly affected by external cycles going on during our period of history. One would not act or react the same today as during different periods of history such as the Revolutionary War, the American Civil War, the cold war or the economic boom since 1982. We also must put our internal cycles in sync with the cycles of the environment; for our purposes, we want to consider the investment cycles.

As we all have different needs and wants, we discover how to get out of life what we are searching for. Some of us go through life in a continual search while others find what they are looking for only to find out later that their desires have changed. Others reach their targets only to create new ones and keep going. There is no limit in your life unless you choose to believe it.

We need to ask ourselves what we want to get out of investing and how those desires will be influenced by the investment cycles. Of course, making money is a very important reason to invest but is it your only reason for making investments? Are you setting yourself up for investment disappointments because you feel that losing is part of your life?

To be successful at investing, you must remove the money from the equation to find out your actual desire. Money should be the end product for investing. If you are looking for excitement then you may very well enjoy skydiving or surfing instead.

Through our journey we all share common experiences. We lose and get frustrated, sometimes feeling lousy, stressed, or disappointed. But the ability to overcome these obstacles is what separates the winners from the losers. I see these as setbacks, opportunities to grow and overcome what is in our way. If we allow these experiences to win then we will never grow. We must learn to get around the factors that could potentially disable us from future growth.

There are four steps to getting what you choose out of life. The first step is to be committed. Being committed allows you to overcome any hardships or setbacks that you have had in the past to achieve your needs. You must stay in the game for what it is that you desire. You don't necessarily remove your obstacles; rather, you work yourself around them to get them out of your way.

The next step is to have conviction on top of your commitment. Here is where the power of positive thinking can propel you to heights that you would never have believed possible. Being positive can relate to not only investing but can be the leading factor in other outcomes, especially as we've seen for athletes. Visualization of where you want to be in your investing cycle, sport cycle, or even your social cycle can lead to endless satisfying results. You must remain positive in your beliefs about yourself and the successes possible in your life.

The third step to achieve what you want out of life is to change your pattern of behavior into new patterns for success. You don't necessarily have to disregard your old behaviors, but recognize that they were not leading you down the path you mindfully chose. If you want to succeed, you need to replace your old behaviors that you understand didn't get you to the destination you desire and replace them with new patterns of behavior that allow you to decisively reach your goals.

Lastly, the new patterns must be applied every day so that they become second nature to you. You must condition yourself to recognize obstacles and move around them. Discipline yourself to follow new patterns of thinking such as positive thinking and visualization of the outcomes you wish to achieve.

These steps can help you through your life cycle, your investment cycle, and your social cycle. But it is up to you to recognize they do exist and can forever change your life.

Winning with the Hand You're Dealt

Our environment and life experiences such as where we grew up, what kind of parents we had, what kind of siblings we had, what kind of life events occurred, what type of cultures we were exposed to, and the relationships that we had (particularly with adults) are all instilled and permanently soldered into our brains. Our subconscious level of thinking operates every moment as we flow through life seeking our wants and needs, as we were sculpted as children into what we are today.

Maybe you were from parents of the Great Depression and they instilled in you ideas that back then made complete sense, but don't fit today's investment climate. As you harbor these handed-down thoughts, they may conflict with what today's reality is signaling. Your parents or your respected elders came from a different life cycle. Remember, the theme here is to identify what cycle you are in related to the current investment cycle.

Childhood experiences can have a tremendous adverse effect on decisions made later in life. For instance, when an investor or trader loses money in the market, she might recall childhood thoughts of being left alone or perhaps being embarrassed in a social situation. The market can stir feelings that could spiral you emotionally down and create self doubt. On the other hand, when you profit from the market, you may remember a time you were praised for doing a great job in the school play or helping a friend.

We all have unique life experiences that we bring to the markets. Your personality is what propels you to follow your life path. Many of these traits were preprogrammed from the day you were conceived. Your temperament is considered a biological and genetic aspect of your personality.

As with your physical traits, your genetic makeup creates your personality predispositions. Therefore, you must be aware of these personality predispositions in order to coordinate your cycles with the current economic or investment cycles.

Also, adverse experiences might have altered your outcome and abilities. For instance, you might have grown taller if it had not been for poor eating habits or an illness. Or, maybe your parents were abusive and did not appreciate you or respond to your needs sufficiently, making you more aggressive toward the markets or others.

I look at personalities as a deck of cards. We are all dealt a hand when we are conceived. Our experiences in our young lives determine which genetic cards will show up. Your hand defines your personality style, and is fairly complete by the end of your youth. The issue that we all contend with is that we all will play the game of life, for the rest of our lives, using our particular and distinctive styles.

We can count on ourselves or other people playing their game true to their personalities more times than not.

We all have the ability to grow and change as adults throughout our lifetimes, but we tend to do so in our consistent and characteristic ways. Our way of being is our personality and this is how we confront obstacles and challenges. Most of us have the ability to deal with hurdles thrown our way. We can adapt to change, which allows us to experience a variety of new possibilities. But, there are those that find themselves up against the wall again and again. These people seem to be locked into rigid and inflexible personality patterns that cause them to have troubled, bored, empty, lonely, or negative experiences repeatedly throughout their lives.

We need to recognize our personality traits and use the positive influences to lead us into productive investment decisions while recognizing the destructive negative forces that hide in our makeup.

Gaining the Investment Edge through the Powers Within

Accordingly, one of the most powerful personality traits is self-confidence. Many great ideas and companies were developed during very difficult times in either the economic cycle or in the individual's personal life cycle.

Self-confident people stand out and become the leaders and the shining lights. They are the attention getters in social or business settings. They have the belief that they are of star quality and give themselves self-respect and self-certainty. They contain a never-ending supply of faith in themselves and a pure commitment to their purpose. Ambition coupled with self-confidence can transform idle dreams into real accomplishments.

The person who is self-confident knows what she wants, and always tries to get it. A major trait of the self-confident person is the ability to attract others to her goals. She is personable to those she meets and she is politically polite. She knows how to motivate a group and lead it to the destination. The self-confident personality has the ability to be more successful than almost any other personality.

The self-confident believe in themselves and their abilities and there is no doubt that they are unique and special. They carry the belief that they are here for a reason. They expect to be treated well by others at all times. They openly express their ambitions and achievements. Self-confident people take pride in effectively selling themselves, their goals, and their ideas to others in order to achieve results. They are able to take advantage of the strengths and abilities of others in order to achieve their goals. They are competitors as they reach for the top and enjoy staying there. They are able to visualize themselves as the star, best in their role, or most accomplished in their game. What I consider a very important trait is that the self-confident person has a keen awareness of her thoughts and feelings with exceptional awareness of her inner state of being. She also accepts compliments, praise, and admiration gracefully. Finally, the self-confident person exudes an emotional vulnerability to negative feelings and assessments of others, which she deeply feels, though she handles it with grace.

We all need to have the joy of being and to believe in ourselves as we encounter an economic depression-style cycle. We should tackle the self-limiting beliefs such as not having enough conviction or not trusting our own judgments. Eliminate the state of mind that is guided by fear, anxiety, and confusion, and stop repeating negative thoughts such as "I'm angry" or "I'm afraid." Keep yourself focused on your goals and desires by not allowing yourself to be distracted from the big picture. If you don't have one, create a personal life investment strategy by utilizing the many tools available to understand the different investment vehicles that will allow you to prosper during the depression cycle. Don't lose your physical and psychological energy because the market's actions look confusing to you. And most of all, if you choose to profit during a difficult cycle for others, don't let guilt feelings overcome you as others who don't have your beliefs or skills will be complaining intensely about not only their investments declining in value but also their businesses and other assets as well.

The power of positive thinking during the most difficult times can lead to tremendous strength when the cycles turn. But, now that we are going into a difficult period of history, we need to understand ourselves and prevent losing and look for winning opportunities. You need to gain the self-confidence to move away from the crowd and ignore the chants that all is okay and we averted the financial crises.

Here's your investment edge. You have the power to wait for opportunities to materialize based on your well-thought-out plan. You have the ability to see the big picture and respond as necessary. You have done the necessary homework and are well prepared to face the other side of this vicious cycle. You have a long-term motive that sees beyond the next few years. Your goal is clearly defined and has highly controlled risk/reward ratios. Most of all, the single variable that engages success is the positive state of mind. Take advantage of your inner ability to get the investment results that you desire, overcome your obstacles, and release the boundaries that inhibit your goals. You may also find your life will become more exciting and rewarding. Unwrap every day as it is a new gift and change your future; the past has been completed.

Part Two

DECIPHERING THE FINANCIAL SYSTEM

Chapter 4

Do Economic Releases Tell the Whole Truth?

A lmost daily, economic releases that are intended to give investors and economists an idea of the state of the current economy make their way into the news. Some of these releases are from government sources and others are from private services that gather information to distribute to the media or as a pay service for subscribers only.

The U.S. Government has the Bureau of Labor Statistics, the Bureau of Economic Development, the Office of Management and Budget, the U.S. Census Bureau, the U.S. Department of the Treasury, the U.S. Department of Commerce, the U.S. Bureau of Economic Analysis, and so on.

Almost every day, traders and investors rely on potentially market-moving economic releases in their decisions for buying and/or selling stocks of different industries or the market as a whole. In this day and age of instantaneous information, markets can move like lightning when the data is released. Sometimes, it doesn't really matter what the economic release is about—it could be just an excuse to move the market so traders have the ability to make a few bucks. Other times, the releases move the markets in one direction for a short period of time until the full release can be interpreted by the traders and the economists to put the reports into context of the economy. Either way, the markets feed on news to move.

The Ripples from a Drop of Data

As an example, early each month, the U.S. Department of Labor through its Bureau of Labor Statistics (BLS) division releases the total number of employed and unemployed persons in the United States for the previous month. Currently this number is closely watched by investors on the morning of its release and can cause large movement in all types of markets, particularly the stock market. It tells us what percentage of the labor force is unemployed. The government conducts a monthly sample survey called the Current Population Survey (CPS) which measures the extent of unemployment. The CPS has been conducted every month since 1940 where it began as a Work Projects Administration project. Since then, it has been expanded and modified several times.

The CPS is a sample of 60,000 households which is estimated to be approximately 110,000 individuals. All of the counties and county-equivalent cities in the country are first grouped into 2,025 geographic areas. Then the Census Bureau designs and selects a sample consisting of 824 of these geographical areas that are intended to represent each state and the District of Columbia. The sample is designed to encompass urban and rural areas, different types of industrial and farming areas, and the major geographical divisions of each state.

Each month, 2,200 Census Bureau employees interview persons in the 60,000 sample households. They inquire about labor force activities such as job holding, job seeking, and the non-labor force status of members of these households. Interviewers gather information from the contact and household members, enter it into their computers, and at the end of each day, it is transmitted to the Census Bureau's central computer in Washington, D.C. A portion of the sample is obtained by phone interview through three central data collection facilities.

The sample may not produce the same results that would be obtained from interviewing the entire population. According to the BLS, the chances are 90 out of 100 that the monthly estimate of unemployment from the sample is within about 290,000 of the figure obtainable from the total census.

But the CPS can be manipulated by the use of seasonal adjustments that are intended to remove the effects of normal seasonal variations such as holidays, school openings and closings, and weather. The BLS explains that these adjustments are used to make it easier to observe fundamental changes in the levels, particularly those associated with general economic expansions and contractions. This can be a grey area and allows for errors in judgment or accuracy.

The second method of sample-based estimates of employment is the Current Employment Statistics (CES) survey also known as the establishment survey. Each month, the CES program surveys about 400,000 businesses nationwide. This survey is designed to provide detailed industry data on employment, hours, and earnings of workers on nonfarm payrolls. The CES is an estimate of nonfarm wage and salary jobs and is not an estimate of employed persons. Individuals with two jobs are counted twice by the payroll survey. And the CES employment survey excludes workers in agriculture, private households, and the self-employed.

The current CES sample survey design has been in place since 2003. The entire sample is redrawn annually and a supplemental sample of new business births are selected midway through the year.

About one-fourth of the sample is rotated out each year and replaced with newly selected businesses. All new samples are done though computer-assisted telephone interview and data is collected for the first five months in this manner. After the five-month initiation period, many samples are transferred to one of several less-costly reporting methods that are self-initiated by the respondent. The CES allows responding businesses a choice of reporting methods such as fax, Web, touch-tone data entry, electronic data interchange, computer-assisted telephone interview, or mail.

But, similar to the CPS, seasonal adjustments can compromise the accuracy of the CES. Here again, the BLS explains that these seasonal adjustments are intended to remove from the data the effects of normal variation from events during the year, such as holidays and weather changes. The CES uses these seasonal adjustments or estimates up through and including the current month's data.

What Revised Releases Tell Us

With an economy the size of the United States', the information gathered from economic releases can sometimes be misleading. Many economic releases are revised and rereleased, showing the inaccuracy of the data in the original version. Why would there be such discrepancies between the first releases and the revisions? And how do we know that the revisions are as accurate as they should be? My opinion from my experiences as a certified public accountant working for one of the big eight firms (back in the 80s there were eight) is that an economy of this scale makes it almost financially impossible to capture all the correct information to filter into the formulas. Remember the famous saying: Garbage in garbage out.

For example, on October 29, 2009, the "advanced estimate" of the real Gross Domestic Product (GDP)—the output of goods and services produced by labor and property located in the United States—for the recently ending third quarter of 2009 was released by the Bureau of Economic Analysis, part of the U.S. Department of Commerce. The advanced estimate was an increase of 3.5 percent, which represents the percentage change from the preceding quarter. For investors relying on this particular number on its first release, it had the illusion of an economy with exhilarating results of growth. This, of course, added ammunition in great hope that a recovery in the national economy is occurring.

Then the second estimate was released on November 24, 2009, almost one month later, and the GDP was revised downward to 2.8 percent. The difference between 3.5 percent and 2.8 percent represents a significant drop of 20 percent. A 20 percent difference in the original GDP estimate of 3.5 percent to 2.8 percent, if reflected in stock prices, would have been quite a sell-off.

Finally, the third estimate and final revision was released on December 22, 2009, for the third quarter 2009 GDP, which came in as a 2.2 percent increase, another percentage change from the preceding quarter. Even the average analyst consensus was for the third estimate of the GDP change to remain at 2.8 percent. The revision from 2.8 percent to 2.2 percent represents a drop of over 21 percent from the second estimate and a whopping drop of over 37 percent from the original advanced estimate of 3.5 percent.

I was on the FOX Business Morning Show with the intellectual Connell McShane when the final release was announced at 8:30 A.M. on December 22, 2009. Minutes before the release as we were waiting for this so-called important number, I was discussing that we really can't believe the numbers and statistics that are being released. I went on to explain that even the brightest minds on Wall Street may be confused as to the actual growth of the economy due to many conflicting series of economic releases that do not add up to the sum of their real parts. When the third estimate was released as another lower revision, I immediately responded that if there was a forth estimate, which does not exist, it could even be revised down further!

The explanation given as to why the data releases are revised by the government was because additional information was not available at the time of the initial publication of the estimate. In reference to the establishment survey estimates, on an annual basis, the establishment survey incorporates a benchmark revision that re-anchors estimates to nearly complete employment counts available from unemployment insurance tax records.

Putting the Numbers in Perspective

Sometimes the data in economic releases causes investors to do a double take, wondering if they read it correctly. How do *those* numbers match up with the current economic environment? I expressed the same thought about not believing the economic indicators during my first appearance on FOX Business's Money for Breakfast show back on May 22, 2008. I pointed out that the unemployment numbers were deceiving and predicted that the economy was slipping into a deep deflationary recession. On that same show I was interviewed by the wonderful and intelligent Alexis Glick where I indicated to her and the viewers to batten down the hatches as I was technically expecting a decline in the stock markets. On later appearances on the FOX Business Network I pounded the table that I was expecting a drop in the equity markets of more than 20 percent and a major rally in the U.S. Treasury market as our indicators were signaling a new cycle low and that turmoil was about to begin in a very bad way for the financial markets, as risk aversion would take over.

Take economic releases with a grain of salt, but further look at the social aspects of the economy as a whole to get a better perspective of the cycle formation. Back in 2008, we were getting social signs that something was inharmoniously occurring in the social portion of the economy and rumors were beginning to fly about trouble in the financial sector. Throughout history, events occur and then generationally repeat themselves and that is unfortunately what investors and the public experience as we go through our lives. The lesson we need to learn is how to survive the ups and downs of present-day economics.

During the 1920s many investors made fortunes only to find themselves broke and falling into poverty going into the 1930s, which we all know as the Great Depression. The positive mental attitudes of the 1920s quickly turned to negative attitudes, and for those of us who have studied the human mind and its emotional powers, it is very difficult to be motivated with negative mental attitudes. It was not only a depression in economic terms but the social state of the people was historically depressed. The dust bowl or drought in the agricultural industry and the policies affecting the economy of the new Federal Reserve were other factors that prolonged the depression.

Don't despair: There were tremendous opportunities that came out of the Great Depression for those who were able to maintain a positive mental attitude. And there will be great opportunities during this deflationary depression, too.

For example, two brothers named Paul and Joseph Galvin needed revenue after the 1929 stock market crash. They had earlier started Chicago's Galvin Manufacturing to sell electric converters for battery-operated radios, but business slowed dramatically. A nearby radio parts company owned by William Lear in the same factory building and an audio engineer named Elmer Wavering teamed together with the two brothers to create the first car radio. They installed the first car radio in a Studebaker in May 1930. Paul Galvin then drove the Studebaker over 800 miles to the Radio Manufacturers Convention in Atlantic City, New Jersey. He parked his Studebaker outside on the pier and played the radio loud because he didn't have a booth inside the convention. Show attendees began to take notice as they walked by and listened to the radio installed inside the Studebaker. Paul received enough orders from that showing to enable the company to survive and get the next growth stage. According to the Motorola web site, Paul Galvin created the name *Motorola* for the car radio that he described as sound in motion from *motor*, representing the car, and *-ola*, which was a popular suffix in those days. Because Motorola became so well known, he later changed the whole name of the company that is today known as Motorola, Inc.

Another great example is that of a sales manager at a local small grocery store in Illinois who envisioned a huge store that would attract customers if there were a variety of goods and discounts. According to www.kingkullen.com, he wrote a letter to the president of the small store where he worked explaining in detail his idea. His letter went unanswered. The sales manager, Michael Cullen, quit his job and moved from Herrin, Illinois to New York where he leased a vacant garage in Queens. He named the new store King Kullen Grocery in August 1930. Unfortunately, he died six years later but by the time of his death he had expanded to 17 supermarkets, and today there are approximately 46 King Kullen supermarkets which are currently privately owned by the third generation of Cullens. The Smithsonian Institute has recognized King Kullen as America's first supermarket.

And again, in 1933, a woman by the name of Ruth Wakefield ran the Toll House Inn in Whitman, Massachusetts. The story at www.nestlecafe.com tells us she used a cookie recipe from back in colonial times called "Butter Drop Do" which called for baker's chocolate, but Wakefield didn't have any. So instead, she chopped up a Nestlé chocolate bar thinking it would melt into the cookie. Instead, the chocolate held its shape and its texture became creamy. The cookie became such a hit and success with the patrons that when the Nestlé Company heard about it they made a deal with Wakefield to print her recipe for Toll House Cookies on the wrapper, which continues to this day on the packages of the Nestlé chocolate chips.

Don't Believe Everything You Hear, Read, or See

I thought of titling this book *Don't Believe Everything You Hear, Read, or See*, but there were so many other facets of economic cycles I wanted to cover, it didn't fit. Those words, however, do fit this chapter: The underlying fundamentals of an economy cannot be scientifically quantified in economic releases.

Markets can at times become irrational and play tricks on our psychology as investors. Sometimes, an economic number is released and the markets react opposite to the way you may interpret its meaning or what you believe should be the result. Let me clarify the word *should*. Don't expect the market to follow the information in economic releases. Look very closely at what the markets are actually doing, especially in the few minutes or even days following a release. There are many traders and investors who actually don't make investment decisions until they view the reactions of the markets, whether in stock, bonds, currencies, or commodities.

Over the centuries, many people have studied the engineering of the markets. One rule of thumb that an investor needs to remember is that the real economy may not be reflected in stock prices on a daily, weekly, or monthly basis. But the controlling of your risk level and the exiting of winning and losing positions in your investments is essential to long-term success in preserving capital when necessary and taking on more risk when suitable. You can profit during any cycle as long as you believe that the market is always right and you remain flexible, jumping on or off trends as they come.

Chapter 5

Accounting Irregularities and Financial Statement Shenanigans

You can never be truly sure that the numbers presented on income statements or balance sheets are accurate. In accounting, there are opportunities to change the numbers to make them look better than they really are. Irregularities can take many forms. There are cash accounting methods versus accrual accounting methods that can reposition profits and losses through recognition and timing manipulation. Then we have the issue of low pay for people working on financial statements, which can lead to poor quality. And we have the fraudsters who continually try to manipulate the process to their advantage. Then we have the creative disguises that create better-than-actual financial statements.

Cash versus Accrual Accounting

Cash basis accounting records transactions that come in and out on the day they actually occur. In my opinion, cash basis accounting is more accurate because it reflects the actual cash flow of a corporation and is easily auditable.

Accrual accounting, which most corporations use, is a method that records money that is estimated or expected to flow into and out of accounts. For example, the most important and closely watched account is the gross revenue line of a corporation. This account reflects sales and growth, and using the accrual method of accounting gives unscrupulous managers or internal accountants the opportunity to commit fraud. The gross revenue line item includes a subaccount called accounts receivable. The accounts receivable amount shows up on the balance sheet in the asset section and is also included as part of gross revenue in the income statement. The problem with accounts receivable in accrual accounting is that it is almost always an estimate of what the accounts are expected to collect. This amount is an estimate because management cannot identify the precise amount its customers or clients actually owe to the business. This amount is less certain than the actual number that may be ultimately collected in the end.

Furthermore, the accounts receivable valuation can go beyond the good faith estimate of the actual collection from the customer or client. This is one area where management can be tempted to tamper with the numbers and have the opportunity to commit a fraud that the investor looking at the numbers would not have a clue about. With accrual accounting, there is no cash yet collected when sales are closed and the amounts waiting to be collected are in the receivables account. Management has the ability to record fraudulent or aggressive sales numbers in many ways, such as recording fictitious sales from fictitiously created customers or clients.

Continuing with accounts receivable and accrual accounting, the accounts receivable and sales revenue line items can be inflated with a method of keeping the books open after the end of the accounting period. This simply means that real sales made in the subsequent period can be recorded in the current year-end financial statements, which inflates the assets and revenue amounts.

The function of an audit is to test the existence and the ability to collect the accounts receivable stated on the books. In theory, the audit is an opportunity to isolate fraudulent practices. But when it comes to very large companies with millions of dollars in accounts receivables and possibly thousands of accounts, the auditing method used is the reliance on statistical sampling. Statistical sampling is reasonable, yet it does not give an exact amount of collectable accounts that are receivable; it is only an estimate.

I will describe other accounting disguises in the last section of this chapter.

A Problem with Training and Resources

As I mentioned in Chapter 4, between 1984 and 1986 I received training from one of the major big eight accounting firms, as they were known at that time. My prior experience as a trader and a Wall Street broker allowed me to be easily recognized by the major firms as an excellent candidate for a career with a big eight firm. My understanding back then was that most accountants at the big eight firms would get experience under their belts and then leave to go work at a Wall Street firm. Very few ever made it to the trading or investment banking side as they desired. Many ended up in the internal accounting departments in hopes of making it over the wall to the sales, trading, or investment banking areas. I wonder whatever happened to some of the colleagues that I knew.

In any event, the criteria set out by the state for being designated a Certified Public Accountant was to have had at least one year of experience in auditing for a graduate degree, which I was pursuing.

An undergraduate degree was required to have at least two years of audit experience to be designated as a Certified Public Accountant. At the time, I was several years out of my undergraduate studies, I had work experience, and I was working with recent college graduates who were working to get their two years of experience.

After I joined the firm, the partners in charge of the audits for some Wall Street firms quickly recognized that my skills would greatly enhance the firm's profile. So, in a flash, I was sent to Wall Street firm audit engagements instead of other fields such as manufacturing, non-profit organizations, and professional firms.

My first auditing assignment was for a major Wall Street firm which not only handled basic stocks and bonds, but also had a commodity futures division. My prior experience on Wall Street was in the commodity futures area, as I originally came to New York to be a floor trader on the New York Futures Exchange prior to joining a major Wall Street firm. I was not only a licensed stock broker, but my specialty of being a licensed commodity broker came in quite handy in this situation.

Here is where the light bulb went on in my head. Before the engagement begins, the audit team meets with the management to get to know each other. It's more like breaking the ice as we will be interacting with them for many months to come. Our first meeting began over lunch and continued afterwards in the offices of the management of the firm. Back in those days, lunch seemed to be the highlight of the day for most accountants. For me, prior to leaving Wall Street, lunch used to be a quick run to the cafeteria or a delivery to my desk as I was watching the market movements for my clients.

In that first meeting, I began to size up the management. My undergraduate degree in speech communications allowed me to read body language and interpersonal communication skills of others. I was even more intrigued by my colleagues from the accounting firm. I was beginning to realize how little they really knew. Of course, they understood the basics of accounting such as T accounts, debits, and credits. But, they had very little understanding of the design and flow of Wall Street products.

Now, here I was, in a meeting with entry-level staff auditors, of which I was one, called staff B. The next levels represented in the meeting were staff As: seniors, supervisors, and the manager in charge of the audit for the accounting firm. The partners of the auditing firm usually didn't come to these introductory meetings, let alone even know the names of the staff members actually doing the audit work for them. They more or less interacted with the managers on the audit to get their details and information.

The audit engagement started. The staff A and staff B auditors were the ones designated to go through the accounts and microfiche to determine that the positioning of an account matched the account totals, which then matched the account groupings by office. This was such an easy task for me that I got most of the daily work assigned to me done by lunch as my coworkers were spending the whole day or even part of their evenings to figure it out. Recognizing my abilities, my coworkers began seeking me out to help them complete their tasks. The audit supervisors were beginning to get frustrated with me as I was completing my assignments in a shorter period of time than what was allotted to me by the audit schedule, which I interpreted as less billable hours. The audit schedule had been in place for years and usually the hours in the schedule were pretty much the fee hours to be collected.

Not only were my coworkers coming to me, but as the audit job progressed, the management of the company that we were auditing took an interest in me and my ability to understand their systems and products. I even remember one of the company's managers commenting to me that "it was about time they sent someone who knows what we do instead of these young auditors who don't have a clue and need training." It even reached a point in the audit engagement that when a level above me asked for some materials from the company's management, they would come and deliver it to me and let me know who asked for it so I could explain what they were looking at.

Now, I'm far from being the sharpest tool in the shed, but when the seniors and supervisors began to see what was happening, egos started to flare. Several weeks into the job I was called back to the main office for a talk at the request of the partner on the engagement. It seems that my experience made headline news in the audit engagement. I was expecting to be told to follow the path of the audit by keeping the appropriate fee hours for billing and not to interact with management as that was not my job. Instead, to my surprise, I was hailed and told I was well respected. The partner was not only impressed by my experience from Wall Street days but also my communication skills.

The partner had also been informed by a manager I had befriended that I was different from all the rest and the firm should take advantage of my talents. Therefore, the partner asked me to put together a training program for entry-level auditors about option contracts and how to audit them. I was proud to do it. I was now reporting directly to the partners in charge of Wall Street company audits.

It got even better several days later. My manager friend set up a lunch with me and another Wall Street partner who wanted to speak with me. During the lunch he went through a list of questions trying to size up me and my experience level. Finally, as dessert came around, I found out why he wanted to speak with me. He pulled out a chart of a British pound futures contract and put it on the table. He them looked at me in a certain way that said to me he was on the wrong side of the market. He asked me to read the chart and make a suggestion on the future probable direction of the British pound currency versus the U.S. dollar. At that moment, I said, "Don't tell me your position, but if you're long, you're wrong." He thanked me for the advice and we rarely spoke or saw much of each other during my remaining year at the firm. Later on, my manager friend told me that he was long.

My conclusion is this: Accountants and auditors—not only in accounting firms but also in other areas of financial and institutional businesses including our government watchdog agencies—are not adequately trained or don't have the adequate resources to hire qualified people to do their job. And their job is to protect the investors and the public from wrongdoings by the people in society that believe that they can get away with it. More money would be saved for the investors and they would become more confident about the watchdog system if the accountants and auditors were compensated at levels that would attract competently trained people.

Why There are So Many Frauds

Based on the previous discussion, you can see that unscrupulous managers have many opportunities to commit fraud. As untrained or unqualified individuals are hired to do the internal accounting or audits, managers can manipulate the books to show inaccuracies as if they are facts. The untrained accountant would not be able to recognize, for example, a false bill or receivable. Their job is to mainly record and audit what they are told to review.

Year after year, we hear about fraud in public corporations where investors relied on financial statements to make intelligent investments. Some of the smartest investors and fund managers in the world have been duped by such frauds. In my opinion, it has probably been happening since we developed the capitalistic stock market concept. But companies today are so large that it is easier to hide and tamper with the books. Companies are now capitalized in the billions (not millions anymore), and also have become huge conglomerates created from the merger mania of the late 1980s and throughout the 1990s.

One of the most recent frauds and one of the largest bankruptcy reorganizations in history was back in October 2001: the Enron Corporation. Enron was an American energy company based in Houston, Texas. I use this example because not only was the company exposed as a sham, taking down its employees as investors and the public investors, but it also took down one of the most prestigious accounting firms in history: Arthur Andersen. The Enron scandal is known as one of the biggest audit failures in recent history. Arthur Andersen, at that time, was one of the largest audit and accountancy partnerships in the world.

Through the use of accounting loopholes, special purpose entities, and poor financial reporting, management was able to hide billions of dollars of debt from deals and projects that failed. It also became known that the chief officers and executives of Enron misled Enron's board of directors and audit committee on high-risk accounting concepts and pressured Arthur Andersen to ignore their concepts of creative accounting.

Another fraud turned scandal was that of Bernard Madoff, a former chairman of the NASDAQ who confessed in 2008. His Wall Street firm, Bernard L. Madoff Investment Securities LLC, has been called the largest investor fraud ever committed by an individual. His business was set up as a vertical company where they were the managers and had custody of customer funds at the same time. The business was known to be one of the top market makers on Wall Street. What was unusual about his business was that it was not a public company, so for auditors he was able to hire accountants who were far from the largest. In fact, he used a very small firm, enabling him to cover up his Ponzi scheme. In its simplest form, he basically made up profits to investors, sent out statements, and used other or new investors' money to pay off investors who were receiving payouts or wanted distributions.

Because of this fraud, the U.S. Securities and Exchange Commission (SEC) came under fire for not taking action or questioning the firm more thoroughly. There were questions raised about Madoff's activities as early as 1999, which were ignored by the SEC.

Fraud in the financial world will continue as long as auditing firms and watchdog agencies hire incompetent, inexperienced, and underpaid people to do the job of protecting the public. Even our leaders in the industry need to take notice when an irregularity is identified and investigate with qualified personnel. If not, then the investing public will lose trust and faith in the system. As part of my predicted deflationary depression cycle, in analyzing the decreasing volumes on the major stock exchanges, I believe that the public may have lost interest in investing in stocks for many years to come due to the frauds that have transpired. Either the investors themselves have lost substantial amounts of money due to fraud or they know someone who has.

The GE Restatement

In January 2007, the General Electric corporation announced that it was restating earnings a total of $343 million lower due to a decision made over five years earlier by the chief accountant of the SEC on how the company recorded interest rate swaps.

According to a Special Note to GE Investors in 2007, GE stated that it had amended its 2005 10-K to restate its financial position and results of operations for the years 2001 through 2005. They also announced that they had amended their 10-Q for each of the first three quarters of 2006 to restate related interim financial statements.

On a prior occasion in May of 2005, General Electric also announced a restating of earnings from 2001 to the first quarter of 2005 after an internal audit found that its accounting for certain currency and interest rate derivatives did not comply with accounting standards. The accounting mistakes made a significant difference in some quarters and reduced earnings the company had previously reported in two of them.

As a result of the restatement, GE needed to make changes to its accounting policies and procedures. Accordingly, the audit committee of GE's board hired its own independent counsel for the accounting restatements. It seems that revenue recognition had been a problem at several GE units.

Due to an investigation, GE announced that there would be some changes in its accounting procedures. Such changes would include additional staff to the corporate accounting department to increase the effectiveness of the internal audit department.

GE had to dig deeper and investigate their accounting issues as an internal investigation was led by WilmerHale LLC's William McLucas, a former head of the SEC's enforcement division where he conducted internal investigations of Enron and WorldCom, Inc.

As corporations become too big to fail, accounting irregularities and corrections are becoming all too common. Most likely it is too costly to control each minute detail of the financials at large companies such as GE and others of comparable size. As a result, from time to time accounting issues will affect the financial statements and we hope that it will not be a company we are invested in at the time. There is really no way you and I as investors can control this kind of risk. That is the job of the watchdogs we rely on to protect us from such events.

Accounting's Many Disguises

In the first section of this chapter, I explained the manipulation of accounts receivable using accrual accounting as an example. Let me continue with a few other disguises that may alter the accuracy of balance sheets and income statements such as accounts payable, prepaid expenses, fixed assets, and inventory manipulation.

Using accounts payable, management can understate expenses, which thereby overstates net income. It can be very easy to detect an understatement of the amount of expenses payable by looking at the subsequent period following the close of the year or period in question. This type of fraud is not very common.

A manager can overstate income and understate liabilities by changing deferred revenue into earned revenue. Deferred revenue is a sale in a subsequent period to the close of the current period of which will be made but will not close until after the books are closed. By bringing this amount back into earned revenue, the management is recognizing a sale before it is actually earned. This is not easy to detect because the sales process is not always clear regarding when a sale is actually fully closed.

Prepaid expenses are expenses that have been paid but are expected to be applied to the subsequent period after the current year end or period in question. Management can understate current year expenses by claiming that certain services are for future accounting periods, thereby fraudulently claiming these prepaid expenses as an asset on the balance sheet, when in actuality they were incurred in the period before the close of the financial statements. When prepaid expenses are accounted for as an asset instead of its proper classification as an expense, the result is that expenses are understated, which thereby inaccurately overstates profits for the accounting period.

Fixed assets, using generally accepted accounting principles (GAAP), have multiple methods of depreciation for their usefulness of life as an asset for a business. There is opportunity here for management to take advantage of GAAP by using various estimates for the life span of the fixed asset. If management understates the depreciation expense by increasing the life of fixed asset, the result is that the firm appears more profitable than it would be if it had used a shorter or more accurate life span for the depreciation expense. Not only can the reduced depreciation expense overstate the usefulness of the life of a fixed asset, but management can also keep obsolete assets or assets that are no longer used in the operation of the business on the balance sheets. By keeping obsolete fixed assets on the balance sheet, the resulting financial statements overstate net income as the losses on the discarding of the fixed assets would never be accounted for.

Finally, the inventory line item offers the best opportunity for management to play with the financial statements. To increase gross profits or operating profits, the value of the ending inventory for the period needs to be overstated. There are a couple of ways that this can be accomplished. Management can state that the ending inventory is higher in value than it actually is. Unit costs attached to the remaining inventory can be inflated, thereby resulting in lower unit costs for the inventory used in the current accounting period, which results in higher net income. Another method of overstating income is to include obsolete and damaged inventory in the ending inventory count, which results in less cost per unit of the total inventory used during the accounting period, again thereby increasing net income as the cost of inventory would be lower.

Summary

From the income statements to the balance sheets, individuals and corporate executives have the ability to present financial statements that, at face value, look great. But in reality, these statements may contain misinformation that you and I as investors rely on in our decision making process. This leads me to emphasize that the price of the stock is just as important as your interpretation of the company you are either invested in or considering. If a stock is moving lower and the financial statements along with comments from management don't agree, then the price of the stock will be your most important indicator. News travels fast and the stock price will most likely reflect future news events about a company that you may not have heard yet or have been able to figure out. Remember, the stock price is always right and the market does not know your position.

Chapter 6

Whatever Happened to Modern Portfolio Theory and Asset Allocation Models?

As the financial community comes up with methods to attract money to investments, the concept of modern portfolio theory lies directly in the forefront of modeling. As stated in this concept's title, it is only a theory that these models will act similar to their historical equations. In reality, nobody really knows the future, but mathematicians come up with models full of past history. One of the assumptions is that the investor will hold on to his investments for a long period of time, which implies smooth volatility of returns. Another assumption inherent in these models is the use of year-end returns. But, inside the years, volatility occurs and is not included in the models.

Using average year-end returns in the efficient frontier model is similar to an anonymous quote I heard recently: It's like putting one foot in a pail of ice and the other foot in a pail of boiling water and on average feeling fine.

As the markets fell after 2007, all asset classes declined in unison as margin calls and liquidation panics ran through the financial community. It is possible that during periods such as manias or deflationary panics, parabolic moves take place and are not usually incorporated into the efficient frontier studies.

In the early years of the investment business, brokers and analysts were usually selling one or two products to their clients, such as equities or fixed income securities. Since managing these products required special attention, clients would have several brokers. One broker would handle their equity investments and the other would manage their fixed income investments. This can be evidenced by the mere fact that many years ago there were boutique firms that had their own specialties. Such specialties included stocks, penny stocks, corporate bonds, municipal bonds, commodities, precious metals, and a whole host of other products.

But over the years the specialty boutique firms had trouble selling their specialty products due to the downward portion of the investment cycle of their products. For instance, equity portfolios declined substantially in the mid 1970s. Brokers had a difficult time calling on prospects and existing clients to pitch new stock investments. Similarly, a precious metals specialty firm's brokers were having a hard time pitching the purchase of gold and silver during the 1990 bull market in stocks when no one was interested in the shiny metals.

The Wall Street firms needed to develop a way to smooth out their revenue streams and not have a revolving door of clients. As clients chased performance, they would leave the firm that was in the declining cycle of their specialty products.

Along came the concept of asset allocation. The purpose of asset allocation was and is to diversify an investment portfolio so that the decline in one particular asset class is offset by the rise of another asset class. An investor can choose from a wide range of investment products for his portfolio and the broker can maintain a more stable book of clients and revenue stream.

In construction of a portfolio, different levels of risk tolerance models are available to the investor. For example, if you have a long time horizon and you want to take on more risk, you may choose a portfolio allocation more toward equities versus fixed income investments. On the other hand, if you are a conservative investor who does not want to see your investments greatly fluctuate, then you may choose to allocate more of your portfolio to fixed income investments than equities. I am not recommending any of these portfolios; I am just explaining the difference in the risk tolerance levels of asset allocation. The problem with the models is that they use past history to mathematically illustrate the risk versus reward. Past history could be the last 20 to 30 years. Unfortunately, as we enter a deflationary cycle, the models have been reflecting results of the bull market which started back in late summer of 1982.

Using these models, investors are encouraged and have the ability to rebalance their holdings, which reallocates their original strategy of the investments in their portfolios. In essence, investors liquidate part of the portfolio investment that had performed the best and move the investment gain to the portfolio investment that had underperformed. In theory, this type of rebalancing works, but, in my opinion, it is not realistic to move some of the investments from a performing asset class to a lower-performing asset class. My experience indicates just the opposite, which would be to hold on to winners and get rid of losers. The brokers' job is to keep the balance in the portfolio based on the level of risk of the investor. Therefore, too much diversification can actually hurt a portfolio as one moves money into a lower-performing investment from a better-producing investment.

With the development of asset allocation models and the merging of boutique firms into individual major firms, brokers were able to satisfy a clientele with multiple investment opportunities. At the same time, investors were educated about the different cycles of many of the asset classes available and were not shaken as much by potentially large fluctuations in the individual investments that comprised their total portfolio.

The premise of asset allocation is based on modern portfolio theory and the efficient markets hypothesis.

The Effect of Asset Pricing Shifts on Modern Portfolio Theory

The history of the efficient frontier uses specific time periods such as the last 20 or 30 years. Different time periods will give different results. The efficient frontier models that are in use today show historical results of different asset classes. But looking at the past 20 years shows that most asset classes increased in value, most notably stocks and U.S. Treasury bonds. During an expected deflationary depression cycle, however, all major asset classes have the potential to move lower as investors sell assets to raise cash regardless of whether the investment class is worthy of being held. In other words, when panic ensues and people need to raise cash, it doesn't matter what the asset is or what class it's in. Panic will override valuation, which pushes prices down to extremely low levels until it subsides. This puts the markets in disarray, which would decouple the fundamentals from actual prices.

Modern portfolio theory pursues the concept that a higher level of risk in an investment has the potential for higher reward or return, and the lower the level of risk in an investment, the lower its inherent potential reward or return. This theory is used to develop asset allocation models to fit the risk tolerance of the investor. The goal is to optimize or maximize the expected return based on the risk tolerance level.

Modern portfolio theory suggests that it's possible to construct optimal portfolios that are expected to return maximum results based on the investor's given level of risk. In order to determine the construction, assets are plotted on the efficient frontier as shown in Figure 6.1.

Now let's compare Figure 6.1, the efficient frontier chart from 1970–2000, with an updated efficient frontier in Figure 6.2 which now includes eight more years. Notice that adding eight years to the model actually decreases the returns. This illustrates that the combination of stocks versus bonds in the models declined in value from 2000 to 2008. As a comparison of the figures shows, following this model, investors most likely lost asset values between the years 2000 and 2008. Most advisors likely wouldn't show you these comparisons as they portray a reversal of fortunes made in Figure 6.1. Going forward, I predict the efficient frontier model will continually show decreasing returns over the next 10 years, and I wouldn't rely on these models for any investment allocation decision. At some point,

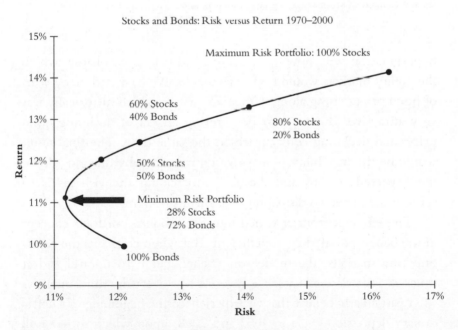

Figure 6.1   The Efficient Frontier, 1970–2000
SOURCE: Courtesy of Morningstar. Reprinted with permission.

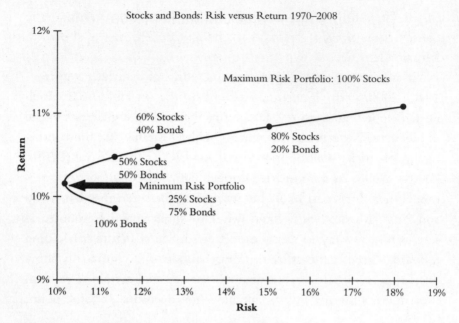

Figure 6.2   The Efficient Frontier, 1970–2008
SOURCE: Courtesy of Morningstar. Reprinted with permission.

hyperinflation will show up, causing bond prices to collapse, which the equity markets would find unfavorable. We have had many years of bond prices rising along with stock prices, which historically was very attractive. But we may be entering an era of declining bond prices and declining equity prices at the same time. The final result would be the possibility of negative returns, thereby dragging down the expected returns and drastically increasing the risk levels to achieve my expected dismal returns. Buyers beware!

The efficient frontier is tied into the modern portfolio concept in the belief that markets are efficient. But when crisis hits the economy and markets, the models and beliefs begin to unravel and at times all asset classes may fall as investor fear overrides fundamentals.

I particularly believe that we experienced the beginning of a deflationary depression cycle in 2007 and 2008, upon which most or all asset classes may fall in value as investors liquidate assets to raise cash.

The Failure of the Efficient Market Hypothesis

The efficient market hypothesis is that the markets trade efficiently and that the prices of assets already reflect all available information in the marketplace. It also emphasizes that prices will instantly change to reflect new information as it becomes available. Hence, the use of efficient market hypothesis ties back to the efficient frontier, which ties back to modern portfolio theory.

But what happened in 2007 through 2009? Were the markets truly efficient? Liquidity dried up; lending came to a halt; markets became violent with panic selling. Did the crisis begin with the collapse in real estate prices or was there another force behind the meltdown that would indicate that the markets are not efficient?

The recent meltdown that we have experienced is not new. Markets have tumbled time and time again through history, as not only economic cycles repeat themselves, but fear and greed among the investment crowd causes manias and panics. My belief is that the markets are not as efficient as the efficient market hypothesis assumes.

As I observed in the recent 2007–2009 volatile and quick-moving meltdown of the stock market, other markets also followed suit. The energies market, metals market, and other major asset classes sold off as dramatically as the broader stock market. The cause for this was liquidation by investors and funds and pure panic about the banking system. The system itself generated the crisis which, in my opinion, falsified the efficient market hypothesis. Under the theory, the disturbances were supposed to come from outside the system and there would be a period to adjust to those disturbances. But in this period of history, the disturbance came from created policies that underlie the financial system itself.

In conclusion, the whole system may have been built on false principles, thereby demonstrating that the efficient market hypothesis may be false. If this is the case, then the next cycle is indicating that most asset classes will be subject to liquidation and lower prices, which may last for many years.

Summary

The key to surviving intra-year volatility is to not rely on modern portfolio theory, which incorporates the efficient frontier, because the markets at times are not efficient. When the markets are not efficient, such as during bubbles and panics, one must always be aware of risk tolerance and take a neutral position to be on storm watch. In other words, if you can recognize that a bubble or a panic is developing, and your uncertainly level is high, stay out until a clearer picture emerges.

If you choose to remain invested during these turbulent times, use the derivative tools available to hedge or reduce your exposure by taking an opposite position to offset potential asset declines. This can be accomplished through the use of Exchange Traded Funds (ETFs), options, or futures contracts. For example, if you have a portfolio of stocks or equities, and you don't want to sell for any particular reason but you notice volatility increasing, you may want to buy an inverse ETF, which is a vehicle that is short the market and has the potential to increase in value as your stock portfolio decreases.

Or if you are an outright speculator, you may choose to buy an inverse ETF to profit from a potential market decline. Options and futures also work in similar fashion as you can either buy put options, which have the potential to increase if the market falls, or sell a futures contract on a particular index to take advantage of a decline. If you are not familiar with these vehicles then I suggest you consult your own investment advisor for advice.

Remember that there are opportunities to profit during all types of markets, and in our modern age of computers and technology, there are more investment opportunity vehicles to give you the leverage to take advantage of up or down markets. Similar to the crash of 1929 and the following several years of market declines, there were a few that made handsome profits from the losses of the average long-term investors who refused to sell until it was too late.

Finally, at the near end of the deflationary cycle, that's the time when you want to change your thinking and move into the concept of inflation or hyperinflation. The vehicles available to take advantage of the downside have opposite cousins that allow you to take advantage of the coming upside inflation or hyperinflation cycle that may turn out to be a bubble in itself. Commodities could be very attractive longer term, once the deflationary cycle is complete. Investors can now, through the use of ETFs, manage their own accounts similar to the absolute return or hedge fund models without the costs. In your own account, you can purchase ETFs that invest in metals, metal miners, crude oil, crude oil drillers, and many more segmented groups. Some ETFs also have leverage where the potential movements can increase at a faster rate than the underlying commodity price, but here again, I suggest you work with a seasoned professional when using such vehicles.

I conclude with my current cycle position that the United States is experiencing a deflationary economic environment. Between 2012 and 2018, my belief is that deflation will have taken its course and the next up cycle will begin. Along with my projection for a peak in gold prices, I suspect inflation should occur around 2020.

Part Three

LEARNING FROM THE PAST

Chapter 7

Fallen Civilizations

I t's been said that history repeats itself, and there's plenty of evidence to show the wisdom in saying so. Profiting in economic storms is about understanding where storms originate. It's about keeping your senses attuned to change and observing your position and the greater society's position. This chapter aims to explore three ancient civilizations in great detail: the Roman, Greek, and Egyptian empires. What did these people value? What was the root of their success and the uprooting that led to their downfall? These questions and more will inform our discussion of modern-day finance theory and the engineering of our market system.

The Roman Empire is a great example of a fallen civilization because of its decline in morals, ethics, and values. As the Roman Empire moved itself through history, complacency, along with the belief that their superpower society would continue on, contributed to its decline. Political corruption, opposition between the senate and the emperor, and constant wars with heavy military spending began to take their toll. The result was high inflation and high unemployment, which eventually seeped into the Roman society economic system and crushed the empire financially.

Ancient Greek society has a different twist to its demise. As well educated and decisive as the people were, their biggest problem was that they couldn't unite. Competitiveness and cultural differences between the peasants and the upper classes were never resolved to bring the civilization closer together. Instead, it tore them apart where they eventually succumbed to attacks from other societies that saw the weakness and capitalized on its presence.

Finally, ancient Egypt was ruled by pharaohs and spread over 31 dynasties. The pharaohs were in charge of maintaining order and warding off potential chaos in Egyptian society. But the country slid into anarchy as one weak dynasty followed another. As the pharaoh tradition weakened, so did the society. Outsiders recognized the weakness growing within the Egyptian society, which opened opportunities for attacks and governance by surrounding leaders. Eventually, military takeover led to the fall of the ancient Egyptian Empire.

This chapter is very important to the United States of America's place in the world today. As the American people begin to divide on policy and encounter political along with business corruption and destabilization within their own government, with ever-increasing deficits, other world leaders may be plotting for the right opportunity to take control of the people and the land. The Romans, Greeks, and Egyptians in the end succumbed to outside forces that eventually controlled their future place in history. If we here in the United States don't wake up and learn from history, we, too, may find ourselves in the same demise as the three historical examples presented here.

Roman Empire

According to Roman legends, Romulus founded the city of Rome from a simple village spread out among the hills in the Italian peninsula near the Tiber River in 753 B.C. It began as a monarchy that was originally ruled by kings who held military and political power, but according to legends, the Romans killed their last king and created a new Republic. The Republic was constantly fighting in wars to grow its dominance in the region. The Republic finally ended in 46 B.C. when Julius Caesar became the dictator.

Julius Caesar tried to create a strong and centralized government despite strong opposition from the Senate. The Senate was a governing body made up of mostly wealthy landowners who were descendants of ruling families since the beginning of the sixth century B.C. In March 44 B.C., the Senate united to assassinate Julius Caesar because they were angered by his overthrow of the Roman Republic. With his death, the Senate's goal was to bring back the old Republic, but instead it started a civil war and as history repeats itself, many men competed for power.

After many years of turmoil, the Senate was convinced that Rome needed a single powerful ruler and centralized government, such as the one Caesar tried to create, in order to restore itself to order. In 27 B.C., Octavian, the grandnephew of Julius Caesar who was also adopted as his son, was given the title Augustus as Emperor and began ruling what was officially called the true Roman Empire.

The term Roman Empire is used to refer to the period in ancient Roman history when Rome and its territories were ruled by autocratic emperors. The Roman Empire officially began in 27 B.C. and ended in 476 A.D., a period of over 500 years. During this period, the empire included lands in western and southern Europe, Britain, Asia Minor, and North Africa, including Egypt.

Ancient Rome, at its peak, was militarily strong and economically powerful. Rome represents today, more than 2,000 years later, the greatness an empire can achieve. But it is also a grave reminder that even the most powerful empires can decline and collapse over time if its greatness is not properly governed for its future. History shows us time and time again that there is a rotation of power that moves from empire to empire, which are today known as countries.

Even though the Roman Empire fell more than 1,500 years ago, it is constantly studied by historians because it laid the foundation of

many of the institutions and ideas that exist today in modern societies all around the world. The Roman Empire also strengthened the
Christian religion, which today touches people all over the globe.
But the Empire, as strong as it once was, also illustrates actions and
attitudes that people might want to avoid.

Historians blame the decline of the Roman Empire on multiple
factors, including political and economic corruption and leadership
that was more interested in personal gain than the welfare of its people. The external causes ranged from diseases and plagues that devas-
tated the population to attacks and defeats from the Germans, Huns,
and various other barbarian tribes, which weakened the Empire's
military and chipped away at its territory.

By 286 A.D., the Roman Empire was just a shell and the Emperor
Diocletian split the Empire into two parts. The Eastern Empire eventually became the Byzantine Empire and the Western Empire in
the end declined into nonexistence. By 476 A.D., the remains of the
Western Roman Empire were finally destroyed after German impe-
rial troops in the Italian peninsula removed the last Roman Emperor,
Romulus Augustus, from power and declared their own king, ending
the Roman rule over Europe. Many historians use 476 A.D. as the end
of the Roman Empire, which was represented by the Western Empire
even though the Eastern Empire called Byzantine continued to thrive
for a while afterward.

Like the Roman Empire before it, the Byzantine Empire slowly
began to decline. In 1453 A.D. the Ottoman Empire seized the
remains of the Byzantine Empire and the Eastern Roman Empire was
no longer.

Decline in Morals, Ethics, and Values

One of the leading causes of the fall of the Roman Empire was the
decline in morals, particularly in the rich upper classes, the nobility,
and the emperors. The growth of immoral and promiscuous sexual

behavior included adultery and orgies. Emperors such as Tiberius kept groups of young boys for their pleasure. Emperor Nero practiced incest and also had a male slave castrated so he could take him for his wife. Emperor Elagabalus forced a Vestal Virgin into marriage. Emperor Commodus had harems of concubines and infuriated the Romans by sitting in the theatre or at the games dressed in woman's clothing.

The lower classes and slaves were also affected by the decline in morals. At religious events such as Saturnalia and Bacchanalia there were sacrifices, vulgar songs, lewd acts and sexual promiscuity. In the Coliseum, acts of bestiality and other lewd and sexually explicit behavior were exhibited to entertain those who wished to observe. Brothels and forced prostitution thrived. Gambling on chariot races and gladiatorial contests became widespread along with excessive alcohol consumption. There was also the practice of sadistic cruelty toward both man and animal in the arena.

Decline in ethics and values had a heavy contribution to the demise of the empire. Acceptable rules or standards for human behavior were declining as life was becoming cheap and less important. Bloodshed became a growing part of the culture, which eventually led to extreme cruelty. The values and basic principles of customs and traditions, which were the leading elements of the ideals and institutions for the Roman people, were reaching the low levels. Perverted views of what was right and wrong were showing up in total disregard for human and animal life, which was a result of a lack of ethics.

Political Corruption and the Praetorian Guard

Another main cause of the fall of the Roman Empire was political corruption and the Praetorian Guard. The Praetorian Guard, the elite soldiers who were the bodyguards for the emperor, gained in power and led to political corruption as they grew to such an extent that this massive group of soldiers decided on whether an emperor should be disposed of and who should become the new emperor. As an example, Sejanus, who was the commander of the Praetorian Guard during the reign of Emperor Tiberius, exercised his powers at one point and sold the throne of the world at auction to the highest bidder.

Opposition between the Senate and the Emperor

The opposition between the Senate and the emperor dealt a strong blow to the foundations of the Empire. The Roman Emperor had the legal power to rule Rome's religious, civil, and military affairs, with the Senate acting as an advisory body only. The emperor retained the power over life and death. The powerful and wealthy Roman Emperors inevitably became corrupt and many lived a morally wrong, misleading, and immoral lifestyle. The Roman people witnessed many instances of opposition between the senators and the emperor. Either the senators didn't like the emperor or the emperors was at odds with the senators.

Constant Wars and Heavy Military Spending

Another main cause of the fall of the Roman Empire was the constant wars and heavy military spending. Steady warfare required heavy military spending by the Empire. The Roman army became over-strained and needed more and more soldiers. To increase the amount of soldiers, the barbarians and other foreign armed forces that had been conquered were allowed to join the Roman army. As such, these barbarians and other foreign armed forces were able to gain knowledge of the Roman style of warfare and military tactics. After serving in the Roman army and learning this knowledge, they eventually turned against the Empire, which led to the ruin of Rome by the Visigoths who were led by an ex–Roman soldier, Alaric.

Failing Economy and High Inflation

The Roman Empire was further weakened by a failing economy and high inflation. Inflation refers to the rising cost of goods over time. If wages rise at the same rate as prices, then inflation is not a problem.

But wages remained flat and some even declined, and the people eventually could not afford to buy as much as they did in the past. The government was constantly threatened by bankruptcy due to the cost of defending the Empire, which resulted in a failing economy, heavy taxation, and high inflation. Furthermore, the majority of the people of the Roman Empire did not share in the incredible prosperity of Rome, which made the distribution of wealth extremely uneven.

The Romans used gold coins for currency but too much gold was sent to the orient to pay for luxury goods, which led to a shortage of gold to make the Roman coins. In Rome, inflation was mostly the result of the government's debasing its money. Roman currency was devalued to such an extent that the people returned to a system of bartering to replace the use of currency. At its peak, silver coins were made completely of silver. The people knew how much silver was in the coin and therefore knew its value. The Roman coins were being debased by putting less silver in them which resulted in less value. By 260 A.D., the silver coin was only 5 percent silver and the rest was less valuable metals. This resulted in the need for more money to buy the same amount of goods before the debasing. Starting in 267 A.D., prices rose 700 percent over the next seven-year period.

Unemployment of the Working Classes

Another main cause of the fall of the Roman Empire was an ever increasing unemployment of the working classes. Cheap slave labor resulted in the unemployment of the working class in Rome who became dependent on hand-outs from the state. The Romans attempted a policy of unrestricted trade but this led to the working class being unable to compete with foreign trade. This further resulted in the government being forced to subsidize the working-class Romans to make up the differences in prices. A final result was that thousands of Romans chose just to live on the government subsidies, thereby sacrificing their standard of living for an idle life of ease. The substantial divide between the rich Romans and the poor Romans increased still further.

The Cost of Gladiatorial Games to Please the Mob

We have all heard about the extravagant displays of the gladiatorial games. Gladiators could be compared to our modern game of football. The unemployment of thousands of Romans created boredom, which led to civil unrest and rioting in the streets. Today, in the United States, we are also experiencing over 10 percent, according to the government statistic, unemployment rates. As this mob-type mentality grew, the government realized that these unemployed people needed to be entertained, which led to the creation of the spectacular gladiatorial games. The Emperors, and therefore the state, and corrupt politicians bore the high costs of the gladiatorial games to show goodwill and encouragement to the mob. Eventually, the popularity of the games grew so big that the costs of producing them came to one-third of the total income of the Roman Empire. Again, today in the United States, the government is trying to implement programs and encouragement to the unemployed by introducing goodwill programs that only seem to please the unemployed, which encourages them to have little incentive to look for jobs.

The Final Collapse

When the Roman Empire collapsed, the highly developed monetary systems of the ancient world collapsed with it, as it was viewed as the leading system. Subsistence agriculture and barter began to dominate the landscape. Money was used only in the small amounts of long distance trade in luxuries that survived.

There were many factors that caused and influenced the decline of Roman Empire. Rome's army became too large as it hired captured soldiers who were not Romans and not loyal to Rome. Trade was constantly disrupted because of wars, which created economic suffering as goods could not be freely bought and sold. As heavy taxes were paid by the provinces to support the luxury of Rome, the conquered people began to resent this structure. Conflict and social unrest was created by the wide gap between the rich and poor.

Slavery eroded the economy by taking work away from the working class. The spread of Christianity divided the Empire and caused many people under Roman rule to reject traditional Roman culture. The Roman society was weakened by its materialism and focus on luxury, especially in the ruling classes. Eventually the Empire became a dictatorship and the people became less involved in the government. Inheritance of the title of Emperor was unstable, leading to power struggles, violence, and insecurity. The division of the Empire into the Eastern and Western Empires weakened the power of Rome. Finally, the Germanic tribes of Northern Europe became strong military forces and attacked the Empire thereby conquering Rome in 456 A.D.

Ancient Greece

Ancient Greece has been known as the root of today's Western culture and modern society's foundation. It had great influence over the world's development like no other civilization had. However, the ancient Greek civilization itself didn't last long. A main reason for its downfall was that its people could not unite.

Similar to regional invading and warlike young potential societies, the classical Greeks settled down to agriculture, forming colonies around the Mediterranean. The economic and social structure was clearly farming, where it had an aristocracy centered on ownership of large estates. Just as tribal soldiers had done in the past, farmers were considered independent by owning their plots of land and claimed their political and social status. As trade developed and the cities grew, the Greek economy rose in social structure and became more complex, resulting in inequalities amongst its people.

Mainland Greece's landscape was rocky and mountainous, which did not make for easy growing of grain. The colonies became dependent on maritime trade. Slaves were seized during frequent wars and colonization, thereby creating a society dependent on slavery, which resulted in less attention to the improvement of manufacturing technology.

The aristocratic character in Greek society, which included politics, was the basis of the importance of the new elite. Even though there were important differences among political groups, the aristocratic gatherings and officials created a single city-state theme in Greek politics. Aristocrats enjoyed the time they had to devote to political life, but it was more about teaching and learning than the political process itself. As for its trade, Greece nurtured its growth, but aristocrats were suspicious of the merchants. Cumbersome coinage was not the least of their concerns.

The bulk of the population of the Greek people was rural and had preserved distinctive rituals and beliefs. The leading political and cultural activities occurred in the cities. Greek farmers gathered annually for a spring passion play to celebrate the recovery of the goddess of fertility from the lower world, which was an important event in preparation for planting that also carried implied hints of the possibility of life after death. This life after death concept was important to many people who endured a life of hard labor and poverty. As farmers attempted to preserve their independence and pay down their heavy debts, tensions developed between the tyrants and the aristocratic conservatives.

As Greek society advanced, farmers specialized in cash crops that required that grain be transported from areas more appropriate for its production such as the northern Middle East, Sicily, and North Africa. The production of olives and grapes, for cooking oil and for the making of wine, spread widely in mainland Greece. Though these products were suitable to soil conditions, they required lots of capital to produce. It took five years before either the vines or olive trees would begin to develop quality fruit. Due to the time it took to develop quality fruit, farmers went into debt and often failed. Wealthy aristocratic estate owners enjoyed great success and in the end they bought up the land of the failed farmers.

By this time, Mediterranean agriculture had become highly market oriented. Few farmers produced just for their own needs, as they did in the early period before civilization fully developed. The empire's goal was to try to access adequate grain supplies and therefore the Greek expansion pushed out mainly toward sources of grain in Sicily and around the Black Sea.

As for the peasant, the importance of commercial farming created a tendency for farmers and their families to come together in small towns rather than the typical villages. These towns developed as trading facilities for grain and other goods. The rural towns remained typical around the Mediterranean even after the classical period had ended.

Despite the unclear status of the merchants, the importance of trade in basic goods created extensive concern for commercial measures whereas a governmental entity may have been needed for all types of trade.

The ships that mainly carried food supplies and other goods were mostly operated by private merchants. But the Greek governments were heavily involved with the supervision of the grain trade by providing transportation services and storage areas to prevent the chance of food shortages. Other items such as pots and tools were sold more widely, and urban artists and craftsmen produced luxury products and participated in the lifestyles of the upper classes. Trading also occurred beyond the typical borders of the Greek civilization for goods that were imported and exported from India and China.

Another key ingredient of classical Greece was slavery. Justification for the necessity of slavery in a proper society was expressed by philosophers such as Aristotle. The philosophy was that, without slaves, how would the aristocrats learn what they needed to learn to maintain a culture or have the time to cultivate political advantage? As slaves were acquired from the results of wars, they were used for household services and as workers in the silver mines. Slaves accelerated the progress of the Athenian empire and commercial operations, but working conditions were extremely poor and appalling. Sparta used helots, or unfree labor, extensively for agricultural work. Of the approximately 270,000 people in fifth-century Athens, 80,000 to 100,000 were slaves, while the helots in Sparta outnumbered their masters by a ratio of nearly ten to one. In some cities, such as Athens, some slaves were allowed to have considerable independence and were able to earn money on their own. Manumission, or freeing, of slaves was very common. But the slave systems did require extensive military command.

The slave system affected the Greek life and certain aspects of politics. Because of abundant slavery, the Greeks were not very interested in technological innovations that would have increased productivity in agriculture and manufacturing processes. But the Greeks did make great advances in shipbuilding and navigation, which were extremely vital to their trading economy.

Tight family structure with the husband and father in control was important in Greek society. Women had economic functions such as involvement in farming and artisan work. Many women with powerful personalities, known as free women, would take over the household and take responsibility for the family possessions, and this was protected by law. But according to the Greek ways, women were inferior in law and culture. Mostly, the activities of free women were directed toward their husbands' interests.

In Greek society, raping a free woman was a lesser offense than seducing her. Though rape was a crime, seducing a free woman meant winning her affections away from her husband and this was thought to be a greater offense. Sometimes in families that were troubled by having too many children, female infants were put to death. Because Greek women were active in business and had the ability to control a minority of all urban properties, their oppression in Greek society was most likely less strict compared to China and other cultures.

Marriages were arranged by a woman's father and husbands were able to divorce their wives at will. If a woman wanted a divorce, she had to go to the courts, which did not make it easy. In Greek society, for men, adultery was tolerated. But, for women, adultery was considered grounds for divorce. The culture even went to the extent that men were able to entertain in separate rooms in the upper-class households. Even though Greek art celebrated the female form and women were represented as goddesses, often with revered powers, the real cultural status of women was low.

Homosexuality in Greek society was accepted. It originated when upper-class boys and girls were often brought up separately, which increased the likelihood of homosexual relations. Most viewed love affairs between young people of the same sex as a normal stage of life. But later in life heterosexuality was emphasized. Older men sometimes took younger partners as a means of training the younger men in sensible wisdom. The Spartans interpreted same-sex relationships as a means of inspiring heroic performance on the battlefields. Homosexuality was mostly prominent among the aristocrats, as male and female peasants and urban workers were mostly together all the time, which by itself promoted heterosexuality.

There were other cultural differences that complicated Greek society. The peasants had beliefs in gods and goddesses but they celebrated separately from the upper classes. The Greek peasants were more interested in the emotional religious practices learned from the Middle East, which were more colorful than the official ceremonies of the upper class. These different beliefs and rituals increased social tensions within Greek society.

In the end, the Greeks' downfall was caused by their inability to unite as one. There were three main reasons that could be attributed to this inability to unite: the geography of the land, the competitiveness of the people, and their extreme personal narcissism.

Geography

Regions were separated due to the jagged coast of the entire area and land broken by bays and gulfs. The interior was full of mountains and mountainous districts. These geographical features caused the Greeks to develop small city-states, which were small nation-like regions built around single cities. These city-states had very little contact with each other and although similar in structure, the people developed different customs, governments, and traditions, which led them to independence from one another, and eventually created separate nation-like cultures.

Competitiveness

The Greeks were highly competitive. There seemed to be an inherent cultural trait to make everything into a contest, from athletics to the great drama festivals. The Greeks even competed in such contests as singing, riddle solving, staying awake, and dancing, all for the satisfaction of the glory. Competition for positions in the government was even fiercer.

Narcissism

It is possible that the competitive nature may have had its roots in the personal narcissism the Greeks possessed. As the Greeks founded the ideology of democracy, individualism began to flourish, where man valued himself as each city-state valued itself. However, this may have gone too far internally, which resulted in personal narcissism. Whatever the reasons are for the personal narcissism in ancient Greek society, it made citizens egotistical to the point of not being able to sacrifice themselves for the city-state welfare of all of Greece. The unwillingness to unite as a nation would be a major cause of their defeat and the fall of their civilization.

An Empire at Odds

There were many factors that caused and influenced the decline of ancient Greece. Conflict and competition between the city-states broke the sense of community in Greece. There was increasing tension and conflict between the ruling aristocracy and the poorer lower classes. Greek colonies around the Mediterranean knew about Greek culture but were not loyal to its meaning of Greece. The neighboring states were increasing in power and were more unified than the city-states of Greece. Different city-states such as Sparta and Athens had completely different forms of government and ways of life. And, lastly, the people became lazy because they were more interested in living the good life than in waging war against their enemies.

Finally, the Peloponnesian War was the turning point of Greek civilization and the start of its decline. Just before the Peloponnesian War, the Greeks faced war with Persia and the Greeks united. This showed that the Greeks could unite. But the heroes of the Persian War were Athens and Sparta, which were both the strongest city-states in ancient Greece; however, they were archenemies. With Athens being innovative and a democratic society, and Sparta being conservative and a monarchy, the rivalry between them was caused by political differences and mutual fears of military aggression.

The Peloponnesian War finally broke out between Athens and Sparta from 431 B.C. to 404 B.C. The war was won by Sparta, but they could not enjoy victory for long as the Thebes, once Sparta's ally, attacked Sparta. After the war was over, the Greeks failed to restore their power and the quality of life declined as a result. Economic conditions deteriorated at a rapid pace and violent clashes between the rich and poor grew more frequent. Public spirit diminished as people grew more self-centered and the city-states lost their strength. The exhausted city-states failed to prevent a Macedonian attack and easily fell to them. This was the beginning of the fall of ancient Greece.

Admired and praised, ancient Greece was once the ruler of the ancient world. The fall of the ancient civilization was from their inability to let their egos go and unite as one. They had always ignored that they could be stronger in unification, as they demonstrated in the Persian War and in later wars.

Ancient Egypt

In our final example of a fallen civilization, ancient Egypt exemplifies what the future may hold for the United States if we don't learn from history. Along the banks of the River Nile, people settled and built houses as they evolved from hunters and gatherers to subsistence agriculturists more than 4,000 years before the Christian era. Egypt grew to become one of the great powers of the ancient Middle East, retaining its dominant position for more than 2,000 years—many times longer than other strong societies that rose in that part of the world. Ancient Egypt is known as the world's first organized society as they developed religion, institutions, and a written hieroglyphic language.

Most of Egypt's ancient history is expressed in numbered dynasties or ruling houses. The three periods of greatest development are called the Old Kingdom, the Middle Kingdom, and the New Kingdom.

The ancient Egyptian people had a bond between the Nile and their institutions. As there was little or no rain, they recognized that there was a natural cycle for the Nile to rise each July and by the end of August the rise or flood would reach its full height. Then at the end of October, the flood would begin to recede, which left behind a fairly uniform deposit of rich silt from the monsoon land of Ethiopia and lagoons and streams that became natural reservoirs for fish. Finally, by April, the Nile was would reach its lowest level. This cycle was repeated every year. Using the rich and fertile silt obtained from the receding waters, the people learned to grow and harvest crops efficiently.

The cycle of the Nile began to convince the people to believe in life after death. The ancient Egyptians gave meaning to the rise and fall of the river as the death of the land followed each year by the rebirth of the crops. Their interpretation of rebirth was seen as a natural sequence to death. They also believed that the sun died when it sank on the western horizon and was reborn in the eastern sky the next morning. These cycles created their belief that humans would also rise and live again, similar to other natural phenomena.

The ancient Egyptians became organized into communities as the draining and irrigating of the fields to grow crops required men to work together. The ancient Egyptian common language was an Afro-Asiatic tongue related to the present day Berber, Cushitic, and Coptic tongues. Racially, the Egyptians were a Mediterranean sub-group of the Caucasoid race.

The early civilization was divided into two parts: Upper Egypt and Lower Egypt. Together they were known as the Two Lands. There was easy communication and contact between the two parts as boats were carried northward by the currents of the Nile and pushed southward by the north winds by the use of sails.

The ancient Egyptians had trade contact with neighboring countries, but also had many indigenous products such as salt from the shallow waters of the Delta and beads of glass. They were practiced in making rope, baskets, and writing material from papyrus. Finally, they made jewelry from the gold and gemstones found in the Eastern Desert.

Around 3100 B.C. the most important political event in ancient Egyptian history was the unification of the two lands: the Black Land of the Delta, so called because of the darkness of its rich soil, and the Red Land of Upper Egypt, the sun-baked land of the desert. The rulers of Lower Egypt wore the red crown and had the bee as their symbol. The leaders of Upper Egypt wore the white crown and took the sedge as their emblem. After the unification of the two kingdoms, the pharaoh wore the double crown symbolizing the unity of the two lands.

The chief god of the Delta was Horus, and that of Upper Egypt was Seth. The unification of the two kingdoms resulted in combining the two myths concerning the gods. Horus was the son of Osiris and Isis and avenged the evil Seth's slaying of his father by killing Seth, thus showing the triumph of good over evil. Horus took over his father's throne and was regarded as the ancestor of the pharaohs. After unification, each pharaoh took a Horus name that indicated that he was the reincarnation of Horus. According to tradition, King Menes of Upper Egypt united the two kingdoms and established his capital at Memphis, then known as the "White Walls." Some scholars believe Menes was the Horus King Narmer, whereas others prefer to regard him as a purely legendary figure.

The ancient Egyptians created a strong, centralized government under a god-king, and the country's emerging economic and political institutions were subject to royal authority. The central government, either directly or through major officials, became the employer of soldiers, retainers, bureaucrats, and artisans whose goods and services benefited the upper classes and the state gods. In the course of the Early Dynastic Period, artisans and civil servants working for the central government fashioned the highly sophisticated traditions of art and learning that later formed the basic pattern of a pharaonic civilization. The unification of Egypt created the foundations of a single state, which in turn gave birth to a new era, that of the pharaohs of ancient Egypt.

The pharaohs of ancient Egypt ruled over one of the oldest and most spectacular civilizations in the world, spanning an astounding period of more than 3,000 years. During this time a succession of 31 dynasties ruled the land, beginning with Menes himself in 3100 B.C. and ending with the last ancient Egyptian pharaoh, Nectanebo II, in 343 B.C.

The pharaohs of ancient Egypt were in charge of maintaining order and warding off potential chaos in the Egyptian society, where the focus was on ensuring the continued worship of the ancient Egyptian gods. They were the head of the military, legal, and religious institutions of the state.

Religion

The ancient Egyptians worshipped many gods and goddesses. Each community or region had its own favorite, and as time passed various local gods and goddesses rose to national importance. Unfortunately, shrines and temples from this era have not survived.

Belief in life after death began early among the ancient Egyptians as they interpreted the cycle of the Nile, and with it began the practice of preserving the body. They preserved bodies by a burial in the dry, hot sand of the desert. With the bodies they buried food and other personal items of the dead for use in their afterlife The wealthy and the pharaohs created tombs instead of graves after techniques of mummifying or embalming the body were developed.

These early tombs were called mastabas: rectangular structures of mud brick with slightly sloping walls. By the end of Dynasty II, the interiors of royal mastabas were being constructed of cut stone.

Later, pyramids were built as monuments to house the tombs of the pharaohs and became the representation of the ancient Egyptian glorification of life after death. As death was seen as the beginning of a journey to the other world, ancient Egyptian society believed that each individual's eternal life was dependent on the continued existence of their king, a belief that made the pharaoh's tomb the concern of the entire kingdom. The first pyramid was the Step Pyramid at Saqqara, built for King Zoser in 2,750 B.C. And 150 years later, in the fourth dynasty of Egypt's Old Kingdom, King Khufu commissioned the building of the largest pyramid of all, the Great Pyramid, which is the last remaining wonder of the Seven Wonders of the Ancient World.

The Decline and Fall of the Pharaohs

During the New Kingdom, Ramses II and his successors were not able to stabilize Egypt out of what was a long and steady decline. This brought an end to the glorious age of the ancient Egyptian pharaohs.

During the twentieth dynasty, toward the end of the second millennium B.C., the Egyptian empire began to weaken from the repeated attacks of Mediterranean invaders known as "Peoples of the Sea," who crossed over from the region of Greece and attacked Egypt from the north, and via Libya in the west. This was known as the Third Intermediate Period for Egypt.

The country slid into anarchy as one weak dynasty followed another. Then, dynasties began competing against each other, which included one founded by priests and another by a Libyan prince. The competition began to tear the country apart. In 667 B.C., the country was invaded by the Assyrians, a neighboring Middle Eastern empire with a reputation for mercilessness and, for a brief while, they controlled the country.

The ancient Egyptian pharaohs fought back and momentarily reestablished their rule, but Egypt was invaded once more. In 525 B.C., the powerful Persian Empire reduced Egypt to the status of a meager province. Initially the Persian rulers respected the customs and traditions of the ancient Egyptians, but as they grew in power they reverted back to their Persian ways and traditions. There were attempts of anti-Persian uprisings which began for a short time from renewed Egyptian independence, but they, too, were finally extinguished by another Persian invasion in 341 B.C.

Alexander the Great

A decade later, in 332 B.C., Alexander the Great, a 25-year-old Greek commander, fought a series of victories against the Persians and heralded in a new phase of the history of the pharaohs of ancient Egypt. He was a brilliant military commander and he wanted to build himself a huge empire. The Egyptians gave Alexander a hero's welcome for liberating them from the Persian rule.

Alexander made the long journey, in Egypt, to the Siwa Oasis to consult with the renowned oracle of Amun. It was considered a highly significant act for the Greek commander, who had dreamed in his youth that he was the son of Amun. Fortunately, his divine birth was confirmed by the oracle. Satisfied, the priests of Amun accorded Alexander the honor of a god, and he was accepted as the new pharaoh of Egypt.

The Ptolemaic Pharaohs

Alexander the Great's career was cut short by a fever in 323 B.C., unfortunately before he ever had the chance to return to Egypt. After his death, the empire he created was divided among his most powerful generals. Egypt was given to his close friend and companion, Ptolemy. At the time, the Egyptians were happy to accept Ptolemy as Alexander's heir and they proclaimed him as their new pharaoh. They did not know that they would eventually lose their independence.

The final chapter of the age of the pharaohs of ancient Egypt came when Ptolemy and the Greeks led Egypt. Throughout ancient Egyptian history, the Egyptians were able to successfully pull themselves out of periods of sustained crisis and reestablished their own dynasties. But it would be a long time before the country would be ruled by native Egyptian rulers again. The Greeks were now in Egypt to stay, and for the next 300 years, it was Ptolemy's rule that controlled the country.

A Downfall Caused by Nature

What is important about ancient Egyptian society is how these people were able to come together and last so long. Part of the bond of its people was from the mere fact that they had a deep-rooted belief in the afterlife.

But through droughts and sandstorms, history shows that it may have been a sudden, unanticipated, catastrophic reduction in the Nile floods over two or three decades that may have caused the initial breakdown of the Old Kingdom, which left the country vulnerable to invasion or a weakening of its monarchy. As the monarchy weakened, it could have allowed for provincial governors to assume royal power over their regions. The reductions in the Nile flood cycle may have created severe famine that gripped the country, thereby paralyzing the political order. There are graphic descriptions of people forced to do unheard-of atrocities such as eating their own children and violating the sanctity of the royal dead. But there is unquestionable evidence that the destructive famine was caused by the reduction of the Nile River flood cycles.

A climatic change that altered the water supply and the lakes along with the Nile River's reduction in flood cycles is considered the force that destroyed the civilization of the ancient Egyptians. A scientific discovery revealed that a pronounced shift in atmospheric circulation occurred account 2,150 B.C., which resulted in an abrupt, short-lived event of cold climate. This also led to less rainfall and a reduction of water flow in the area extending from Tibet to Italy. It is believed that this had catastrophic effects on early state societies and the Egyptian Old Kingdom.

Today, the Nile River is regarded as the source of life in Egypt. The cycles and long-term variations in the Nile floods are beyond the perceptions of people, similar to investing in the markets. It is hard to perceive change of cycles, especially when they are long term and hard to detect. The detection is more of an acceptance factor and this is where most people have the greatest difficulty. Just like the Nile River, which has prosperous times, such as in the Old Kingdom, the stock market has had prosperous times as well. But in order to have prosperous times, there must be a time in a cycle when it turns to a non-prosperous time period. Just like the Nile River, the markets are temperamental and one must accept the fate of the markets to determine opportunities. In the markets, cycles can last from five minutes to decades, such as the one Japan is currently experiencing, which resulted in their market cycle peak in 1990. It is possible that the stock market peak in the United States for the current cycle may have occurred in 2007. Time will tell how long this downward cycle will last, but as history does repeat itself, I predict that we are currently on the other side of a peak cycle that could last for a long time.

Why Look at History?

I have included a short history of the Roman Empire, ancient Greece, and the ancient Egyptian societies because of important lessons that can be taken from their downfalls. Each one being unique, they had their flaws that led to a conclusion of not only their societies but of their powers. A decline in morals and ethics and a complacent people can lead to internal destruction that weakens the defenses, such as in the Roman Empire. In ancient Greece, competitiveness, narcissism, and an empire at odds within itself reveal opportunities to other societies for invasion. Finally, dynasties cannot last forever as they weaken over time from generation to generation, as ancient Egyptian history reveals.

In our current society here in the United States, I see signs of weakening that, if not recognized by our leaders, could leave us open to attack, both militarily and economically. September 11, 2001 was a major attack on our country that demonstrated to the world that we are vulnerable. Since then, there have been other attempts, but because of our brave men and women in homeland security, they have so far been thwarted.

However, currently I see similarity in such areas as decline in moral values and ethics. Fund managers are stealing money from their investors using Ponzi schemes, and high-level governmental and corporate leaders have succumbed to moral and ethical temptation in either their personal or business activities. The role of competitiveness can be rewarding but not to the extent of life or death. And political positions should have term limits to decrease complacency and guard against a weakening political system.

Due to these similarities with previous history, my posture in this continuing economic storm is to stay defensive and nibble. We don't know what is around the corner, but staying defensive and using alternative investment vehicles to either hedge your current positions or take outright bets is what I'm suggesting here. A good idea is to bet against the herd.

Chapter 8

The History of the U.S. Banking System

A review of the banking system in the United States reveals that there have been, and continue to be to this day, questionable policies and corruption issues. The Bank of North America, the first government-incorporated national bank, ended when too much international influence corrupted the bank. The creation of the First Bank of the United States, which was proposed by then Secretary of the Treasury Alexander Hamilton, had trust issues between the South and the North which led to its demise. The Second Bank of the United States, which was designed by then President James Madison to revive a central bank concept, lost its authority as the depository for federal income tax revenue deposits after an official investigation uncovered fraud and corruption. After the Second Bank of the United States failed, the period following was one of free banking which allowed each state to come up with its own act to charter banks. The National Bank Act of 1863 established a system of national charters for banks for its main purpose: the development of a national currency based on bank holdings of U.S. Treasury securities. The current Federal Reserve Bank has been in effect since its establishment in 1913, but as of late is under tremendous scrutiny as its policies haven't been able to smooth out economic manias and depressions. After reviewing the history of the U.S. banking system, I conclude that the current Federal Reserve Bank may not be operating in its current form near the bottom of the deflationary depression cycle that I have been discussing throughout this book. What form the future Federal Reserve Bank will take will depend on the depth and monetary destruction and how many Americans are affected. Citizen unrest may ultimately take its role in the overhaul process. I specifically wrote this chapter to enlighten you on the historical challenges the banking system has faced since our nation's birth, but also to teach you that the current system, though it looks like it's working at times, has inherent flaws that cannot be overlooked going forward if the United States is to stay on a course of solid economic and social growth.

Established in 1694, the Bank of England, formerly known as the Governor and Company of the Bank of England, acts as the central bank for the United Kingdom. The bank has been and is a model on which central banking systems around the world have been designed over many centuries. The bank was originally privately owned and operated until it was nationalized in 1946. Nationalization of the Bank of England's assets meant that it was no longer in private hands and it became a public entity owned by the government. This enabled the government to take responsibility for meeting any debts incurred by the bank.

In 1997, the bank was changed to an independent public organization, which gave it operational independence and the ability to set monetary policy such as interest rates to meet the government's stated inflation target, but it is still wholly owned by the government.

Bank of North America (1782–1785)

The American Revolution, also known as the War of Independence, began when the British Empire imposed a series of taxes to be paid by the colonies in North America for costs associated with keeping them with the Empire. Forced taxation became increasingly unpopular with the colonists because they believed that they lacked elected representation in the British Parliament.

British mercantilist policies, in the form of taxes, were imposing trade restrictions and limiting growth in the new American economy, allowing the British merchants to profit at the new colonial merchants' expense. By 1772, a movement was being established in most of the American colonies to create Committees of Correspondence which eventually evolved into the Provincial Congress.

On December 16, 1773, colonists, as a sign of rebellion against the taxes in the British colony of Boston, Massachusetts, boarded the anchored ships in the Boston Harbor. Their purpose was to destroy the cargo of tea by throwing it into the harbor after officials refused to return three shiploads of taxed tea to Britain as requested. The Boston Tea Party, as it is known today, was the culmination of a resistance movement throughout British America against the tea tax imposed by the British Parliament. Colonists objected to the Tea Act because they believed that it was a violation of their rights to be taxed by a government in which they had no elected representation.

The British Parliament immediately took action by closing Boston's commerce until the British East India Company had been repaid for the destroyed tea. In 1774, the Provincial Congresses spoke up and began to reject the British Parliament's actions. This led to the coordinated effort to create the First Continental Congress to represent the colonies, which officially petitioned the British monarch for repeal of the tea tax and other acts. Resistance began to grow and disagreement became strong, which led to the beginning of the Revolutionary War near Boston in 1775.

In 1775, the British Empire responded by sending combat troops loyal to King George III to the American colonies. As fighting broke out, the colonies quickly mobilized their own troops. The First Continental Congress again tried to appeal for the King's royal intervention on their behalf with Parliament. Unfortunately, that worked against the American colonies, with the King proclaiming a state of "open and avowed rebellion" in a Proclamation in August 1775.

In 1776, representatives from each of the original thirteen states voted unanimously in the Second Continental Congress to adopt a Declaration of Independence that rejected the British monarchy and the British Parliament. It also established the United States as a representative government selected by state legislatures. Finally, in 1781, two main British armies surrendered to the Continental Army, which created a victory in the war for the United States. Thus the United States was born.

In early 1781, the Second Continental Congress reformed to become the Congress of the Confederation and ratified the Articles of Confederation and Perpetual Union in order to allow Congress the power to emit bills of credit. That same year, the Second Continental Congress passed an ordinance to incorporate a privately subscribed national bank.

As a result, the first government-incorporated national bank began in 1782 and was called the Bank of North America. Its design was similar to the structure of the Bank of England and it was located in Philadelphia, Pennsylvania. The idea was conceived by Robert Morris, who was appointed superintendent of the new Department of Finance in 1781 by the Continental Congress. The bank was created to give financial aid and prop up the value of the government's Continental currency and bills of credit that had been used to finance the American Revolution, which were greatly depreciating.

During the years of the bank's operations, objections arose regarding its intended role as a nationwide central bank and its ownership. It was perceived to have too much foreign influence. The discovery of questionable credit favoring foreigners and creating unfair competition against less corrupt state banks issuing their own notes was too much for the people to handle. Pennsylvania even went as far as to repeal its charter to operate in the state in 1785.

The First Bank of the United States (1791–1811)

In 1790, the first Secretary of the Treasury, Alexander Hamilton, proposed to the first session of the First Congress the concept of a central bank to replace the thirteen individual colonies' own banks, currencies, financial institutions and policies. The new proposed bank would handle the financial needs and requirements of the central government of the newly formed United States. As a result and four years after the ratification of the Constitution, the government adopted another central bank called the First Bank of the United States. The new bank was chartered by the U.S. Congress on February 25, 1791. The charter was to last 20 years.

As the bank had support and origin in and among the Northern states, it was seen with suspicion by the representatives from the Southern states. Accordingly, the Southern states' industries, which were mostly agricultural, believed they did not need a centrally concentrated bank. As we now know through history, the suspicion of the Southern states about the motives of the Northern states particularly about banking was not the only disagreement between the two.

Under President James Madison, a bill to recharter the bank failed in the House of Representatives by one vote on January 24, 1811. The bill finally failed in the Senate on February 20, 1811, therefore the First Bank of the United States charter expired that same year. But Madison had a plan to revive the bank.

The Second Bank of the United States (1816–1836)

In 1816, President James Madison revived the central bank concept of the First Bank of the United States and chartered the Second Bank of the United States. Located in Carpenters' Hall in Philadelphia, where the First Bank had been, the Second Bank had branches throughout the United States.

Due to new circumstances, the same congressmen who in 1811 voted not to renew the charter for the First Bank of the United States voted to charter the Second Bank of the United States. Because of the War of 1812, the United States was experiencing severe inflation, debt, and difficulty in financing its military operations, which led to the charter for the Second Bank of the United States. At this point in history, the United States was at its lowest level of credit worthiness and its highest level of borrowing needs since its Declaration of Independence.

In 1816, a charter was approved for 20 years for the Second Bank of the United States. The new bank seemed to have a strong relationship with the federal government and gave it access to profits which did raise concern about its perceived independence. The bank was the main depository institution for the federal government's revenues, which led it to become a political target of outspoken banks chartered by the individual states who also objected to its relationship with the central government.

The United States experienced an economic boom in 1816, despite its debt from the War of 1812, which ended in 1816. This economic boom was a result of the European agricultural industries' devastation from the effects of the Napoleonic Wars. Those results allowed the U.S. agriculture industry to expand and fill the void. As a result, the Second Bank of the United States expanded its lending to aid the boom, which caused major speculation in land. The bank basically practiced the idea of free money lending by allowing almost anyone to borrow money and speculate in land. This overspeculation caused land values to rise to tripling levels. During this boom period, as with most periods when prosperity is in abundance, it was not noticed that widespread fraud was materializing at the bank and that a huge economic bubble was being created. As a theme throughout this book, it's important to note this as another example of history repeating itself. What was happening back in 1819 occurred again in our current modern age banking system and recently ended with a bursting of a real estate bubble in 2007.

National bank managers began to ring the alarm and realized the bank's overextension in the summer of 1818 and started calling in the loans and actually instituted a policy of contraction. As a result, the recalling of loans reduced land sales dramatically. At the same time, Europe's agricultural industry began a quick recovery, which had a direct impact on the United States as the production boom slowed significantly, ending with the Panic of 1819.

The Panic of 1819 is considered the first major financial crisis in the U.S. banking system. In earlier years, the United States experienced a depression in the late 1780s and another severe economic downturn in the late 1790s but those were caused primarily by an economic downturn in the global economies as a whole. But the Panic of 1819 was largely caused by widespread foreclosures, bank failures, unemployment, and a decline in agricultural and manufacturing industries within the United States. The panic ended the economic expansion that occurred after the war of 1812.

It took years for the economy to heal after the Panic of 1819. President Jackson began to despise and question the motives of the current Second Bank of the United States due to the uncovering of fraud and corruption. Therefore, in 1830, he began an official investigation of the bank and as a result he claimed "beyond question that this great and powerful institution had been actively engaged in attempting to influence the elections of the public officers by means of its money." In 1832, four years before the bank's charter was to expire, President Jackson vetoed a re-chartering bill that passed through Congress. As he vetoed the bill, his message was common among citizens as he attacked the mostly rich and foreign stockholders of the bank.

In 1833, President Jackson instructed the Secretary of the Treasury to deposit federal tax revenues into state banks and not into the Second Bank of the United States. The major source of deposits for the bank was U.S. tax revenues and due to this loss it soon began to lose money. Desperate to save itself, it called in all its loans and entirely stopped issuing new loans. After a while, the Second Bank of the United States was left with little money and after its charter expired in 1836, it turned into an ordinary bank in Philadelphia that five years later went bankrupt.

The Free Banking Era (1837–1862)

Beginning in 1837, there were only state chartered banks. This was the beginning of the free banking system which, at the time, did not require a centralized bank. State chartered banks issued bank notes against particular gold and silver coins. States regulated the banks' reserve requirements and interest rates for loans and deposits. They also regulated the banks' capital ratios. I note here that this is similar to the regulations today in the insurance industry. States regulate insurance carriers as to their reserve and capital requirements, among other regulatory issues.

Each state tried to come up with its own act to charter banks. In 1837, Michigan created the Michigan Act that allowed banks to be automatically chartered without the special consent of the state legislature if they fulfilled the state's requirements. This allowed for the creation of unstable banks due to the lack of direct state supervision in the states that adopted the act. When a bank, automatically chartered under the Michigan Act, issued bills, they were perceived to have lower face value. The amount of the discount was determined by the bank's actual financial strength.

At the beginning of the free banking era in 1837, there were 712 chartered banks. This compares to 24 chartered banks in the United States in 1797. In the era, the average life span of a chartered bank was five years. Approximately half the banks failed while a third of them went out of business due to their inability to redeem their notes.

Could you ever believe that there was a time in the United States when there was no central bank, no so-called Federal Reserve nor a Bank of the United States? Most of us today only know the Federal Reserve because it has been around as long as we have been alive. But after the Second Bank of the United States charter expired, no new centralized bank was created to replace it.

The result of what I call previous banking systems experiments left the country once again in a financial meltdown known as the Panic of 1837. I note at this point that history again repeats itself. Not even 20 years had gone by and the country was experiencing another financial panic similar to the panic in 1819 in the previous era.

The veto for renewal for the Second National Bank of the United States by President Jackson in 1836 opened the doors for state banks to take advantage of the current conditions as new banks came rapidly into existence and banking facilities were extremely increased. By midsummer 1836, wild speculations fueled the expansion of foreign goods that were heavily imported and government land sales soared. As paper money was pouring into the Treasury, the Secretary of the Treasury became very concerned about the speed of the speculation and required payment for government lands to be made in gold and silver after August 15, 1836. As is turns out, he was right and because of his actions the gold and silver failed to appear. The effect of the Secretary of the Treasury's requirement immediately was recognized and the level of speculation that existed disappeared. The banks began calling in their loans and property prices fell into a general decline which in turn created the business crash and Panic of 1837.

Along with the expansion of credit by banks, availability of easy money for land speculation, and unfavorable balance of trade in which imports exceeded exports, other reasons contributing to the Panic of 1837 were large state debts due to construction of canals and railroads and crop failures in 1835–1837.

During the first three weeks of April 1837, it has been recorded that 250 businesses failed in New York. Throughout the country, businesses such as mercantile interests, mechanics, farmers, and even laborers experienced disastrous consequences. Bankruptcy and forced sales of merchandise contributed to states that partially or fully failed, and even our general government could not pay its debts as trade stopped quickly and businesses lost confidence.

As one of the results of the Panic of 1837, the banking system suffered a general collapse. Accordingly, out of 850 banks, 343 closed entirely and 62 failed partially. A long period of depression followed for years and the number of banks, after increasing to 901 in 1840, declined to 691 by 1843.

Finally, to build confidence in the banking system during the free banking era, a few local banks stepped up and functioned as the central bank. Several states sought to curb the power of banks in one way or another. In New York, the New York Safety Fund, which was established in 1829, provided deposit insurance for member banks. In Boston, the Suffolk Bank, established in 1818, guaranteed that bank notes traded at near par value and also acted as a private bank, but not a clearing facility.

National Banks (1863–1913)

On February 25, 1863, the National Bank Act of 1863 established a system of national charters for banks as this act became U.S. federal law. One of the main purposes of the act was the development of a national currency based on bank holdings of U.S. Treasury securities. At the same time, the National Bank Act of 1863 established the Office of the Comptroller of the Currency as part of the Department of the Treasury. The purpose of the Office of Comptroller of the Currency was to establish a national security holding department for the execution of the monetary policy along with supervision of the national banks. The Office of the Comptroller of the Currency printed the notes to ensure uniform quality and prevent counterfeiting. The National Bank Act, along with Abraham Lincoln's issuance of "greenbacks," raised money for the government in the American Civil War by requiring national banks to back up their notes with U.S. securities. "Greenbacks" were

U.S. notes, also known as legal tender for all debts, that were issued from 1862 to 1879.

In 1864, the National Bank Act of 1863 was proved to be defective and was replaced by the National Bank Act of 1864, which authorized the Office of the Comptroller of the Currency to examine and regulate nationally chartered banks.

On March 3, 1865, a later act was passed to impose a tax of 10 percent on the notes of state chartered banks, which took effect on July 1, 1866. The purpose of the tax was to effectively force all nonfederal currency from circulation and also force most banks to convert to national banks. There were 1,500 national banks in 1865. By 1870, there were 1,638 national banks and only 325 state chartered banks. Over time, the state chartered banks began to reinvent themselves, even as the tax continued into the 1880s and 1890s, by the creation of the checking account. By creating the checking account, the state chartered banks had, by the 1890s, 90 percent of the money supply. They were making a comeback.

But there continued to be problems in the banking system. The first problem that kept reoccurring was from the requirement that the banks back up the currency with U.S. Treasuries. When the prices of the Treasuries fluctuated in value, banks had to recall loans or borrow from other banks or clearinghouses to keep within capital regulation. In other words, they had to mark to market the Treasuries on their books. The second problem was that of seasonal spikes in withdrawals. A rural bank would have deposit accounts at a larger bank that it would withdraw when the needs were highest, such as when farmers took out money for the planting season. Many banks were badly mismanaged. During the fall, businesses needed to withdraw money from their banks to pay farmers for the purchase of crops. As banks would have to pay out from their reserves, some found themselves without enough reserves to meet withdrawals and had to close. Some of these banks could have been saved if they could have quickly converted their loans into cash. Between the first problem of mark to market and the second problem of seasonal demands, when demands became too big, the bank had to find other sources of lenders to replenish the banking requirements.

There was a great period of industrial growth and expansion between the Civil War and the First World War. But this growth was interrupted many times by financial panics and depressions, which caused banks to fail, stock prices to collapse, and business firms to fail. It seems to be part of the natural cycle of economics. One can never get the money supply exactly correct. Nor can one time speculator and investment emotions with precise timing. Waves of growth panics were followed by depressions, evident by low industrial production and high unemployment. Throughout my research, I continue to conclude that the weakness of the banking system is partially to blame and has intensified depressions after they began.

Liquidity issues lead to crises such as bank runs, which cause severe disruptions and depressions. The Panic of 1907, also known as the 1907 Banker's Panic, became a wake-up call for a serious look at the banking system.

Of course there were economists and businesspeople who tried to warn that there were problems on the horizon, similar to the warnings heard in our most recent years from 2000 to 2007. Back in early 1907, Paul Warburg, a partner of Kuhn, Loeb and Company, published a reform plan titled "A Plan for a Modified Central Bank" in the *New York Times Annual Financial Review* where he outlined a solution that he thought could avert a panic. Also, to follow up on this plan, Jacob Schiff, the chief executive of Kuhn, Loeb and Company, gave a speech to the New York Chamber of Commerce where he warned that "unless we have a central bank with adequate control of credit resources, this country is going to undergo the most severe and far reaching money panic in its history." The Panic of 1907 occurred in October.

The Panic of 1907 is said to have been triggered by a failed attempt to take over the stock of the United Copper Company in October 1907 by the founder of the company and his brother. The brothers realized that there was a large amount of short sellers and traders who had borrowed the stock to sell short to other investors as they were predicting that the stock would fall further. The brothers decided to borrow quite a bit of money from the banking system and aggressively purchase the stock in the open market. Their scheme was to force the short sellers to repay the borrowed stock by buying back the stock at much higher prices of which the brothers planned on selling back to them.

But the brothers both seemed to have miscalculated how much of the company stock was controlled and available by the family because when the short sellers and traders were forced to buy back the stock, they were able to find it from other sources.

This is when the market traders in the stock realized that the plan had failed and the price of United Copper collapsed. The stock dropped so much that the depositors of the banks that had lent the brothers the money began to rush to take their money out of the banks involved. As the panic spread, money was withdrawn from banks associated with the family and spread even further to the trust companies related to those banks. In the end, the share price of United Copper never recovered and in 1913 the company was placed in receivership.

As you can see, this is why the Panic of 1907 was also known as the 1907 Bankers' Panic. J. P. Morgan brought together leading financiers and banks to bail out the panic situation.

After the Panic of 1907, as the United States was the last major country without a central bank, it was widely felt that it might be time to create an institution to provide stability and emergency credit in times of need such as financial crisis. The biggest concern was that by having a decentralized banking system, that there was no satisfactory way for the system to regulate itself and therefore required extraordinary intervention by one institution. Financial leaders were advocating a new central bank with an elastic currency power that could expand or contract the money supply as needed. The next year, Congress established a commission of experts to find a nonpartisan remedy.

This new commission was called the National Monetary Commission, and led by Rhode Island Senator Nelson Aldrich, the Republican leader in the Senate, they set out to Europe to study the central banks of Britain and France. They realized that these central banks were instrumental in the handling of the stabilization of the overall economy and the promotion of international trade. This led to a plan in 1912 to bring central banking back to the United States, where financial stability and expanded international roles were to be controlled by impartial experts, and there would be no political interference or meddling in the financial decisions of this institution.

Aldrich proclaimed that this new central bank had to be on its own, with its own decision-making policies, or it would be attacked by politicians and bankers as had the First and Second Banks of the United States in the past. He came up with the concept of a regional central banking system. President Woodrow Wilson added to this by suggesting that the regional banks be controlled by a central board appointed by the president of the United States.

The bill was introduced and hit great controversy, but in the end everyone seemed to be pleased. After a great debate, the result was that the Federal Reserve currency would become the liability of the U.S. government rather than private banks, and there would be a provision for federal loans to farmers. President Wilson had to assure southerners and westerners that the system was decentralized into 12 districts and that decentralization would weaken New York City's Wall Street influence while strengthening the farther areas of the country. Congress passed the Federal Reserve Act in late 1913. President Wilson signed the Act into law in December 23, 1913.

The Federal Reserve System (1913–Present)

As the Federal Reserve was evolving during World War I, Paul Warburg, the leader of the Federal Reserve, and governor of the Federal Reserve Bank of New York Benjamin Strong convinced

Congress to modify its powers. The result was that the Federal Reserve Bank was given the power to create money of last resort to prevent a downward spiral of withdrawals or withholding of funds, which could create a monetary panic. At the same time, it was also given the power to destroy money in order to slow down excessive growth and speculation.

Even in the 1920s, the Federal Reserve was still experimenting with different approaches for increasing the money supply and decreasing the money supply. Due to the lack of history, these experiments helped create the late 1920s stock market bubble. In 1928, Strong, who was a major influence in the new system, died, which left a tremendous void in Federal Reserve governance, and the bank did not have a chance to realign itself internally in time to understand or react to the 1929 crash. Due to Strong's death, the power void in the decision and policy process left the remaining policy makers to make erroneous decisions, adopting a restrictive policy that added fuel to the crash.

In the formation of the current Federal Reserve system under the Federal Reserve Act, the country was divided into 12 Federal Reserve District Banks with branches. The Federal Reserve Bank serves the 12 district banks. The system is controlled by a Federal Reserve Board whose official name was changed to the Board of Governors of the Federal Reserve System in the Banking Act of 1935. The Board is composed of seven members, who are appointed by the president of the United States and must be confirmed by the U.S. Senate. The president of the United States also appoints the chairman and the vice chairman of the board, who also need to be confirmed by the U.S. Senate. The system is designed to provide a uniform monetary policy, which is administrated by the officers and directors of the 12 district banks and their branches to be reactive to the special needs and conditions of different areas of the United States.

Each District Federal Reserve Bank has a board composed of nine members. By law, the directors are chosen from outside the bank and are proposed to represent business interests within their Federal Reserve Districts. The member commercial banks in the district elect three directors representing the commercial banks that are members of the Federal Reserve System and they elect three members that represent the public. The Board of Governors appoints the last three directors and selects one as the chairman and another as the deputy chairman. The nine directors nominate a president and first vice president of the District Reserve Bank who must be approved by the Board of Governors.

Furthermore, each branch of a District Reserve Bank has its own board of directors comprised of between three to seven members. A majority of the directors are chosen by the branch's District Reserve Bank and the remaining are chosen by the Board of Governors.

The Federal Reserve Bank established a new, centralized system for holding required bank reserves. It also developed a new plan for issuing official currency. Finally, the system allowed individual member banks to borrow from the Federal Reserve Banks as needed to keep liquidity in the banking system in times of stress. All existing national banks were required to be members of the Federal Reserve System, but state chartered banks could become members if they chose to enter and only if they met certain conditions.

The Federal Reserve Bank was now in control of the U.S. money supply through its Board of Governors.

The reserve deposit that a bank must hold at the District Federal Reserve Bank is called the "required reserve." The amount held by a bank at the District Federal Reserve Bank above the reserve amount required by law is called "excess reserves." The reserve requirements percentages can vary within broad limits as decided by the power given to the Board of Governors.

Under the new system of banking, the national banks had to move their maintained deposits of reserves, held either in currency and coin from their own vaults or in the form of deposit claims on other banks, to their district Federal Reserve Bank, and in turn they received deposit credits on the books of the district bank. The required reserve deposits must be equal to a certain percentage of a bank's demand deposit liabilities and time and savings deposits as decided by the Board of Governors.

If a member bank cannot meet its reserve requirement, then it has the ability to borrow from its district Federal Reserve Bank. The member bank can borrow by depositing U.S. securities or loans made to businesses by the bank. The district Federal Reserve Bank gives the bank credit in its reserve deposit account. The bottom line is that the district Federal Reserve Bank gives the bank a loan against the deposit as a credit to draw upon in its reserve account. In effect, the district Federal Reserve Bank liquefies a nonliquid asset by exchanging liabilities with a member bank. The member bank now owes the district Federal Reserve Bank due to the loan and the district Federal Reserve Bank owes the member bank the deposit used as collateral for the loan.

This loan that the member bank borrows from the district Federal Reserve comes with interest. The interest rate charged by the district Federal Reserve Bank to the member bank is called the "discount rate." The Federal Reserve banking system can vary this rate to make it more profitable or less profitable for banks to borrow. This is one method the Federal Reserve Bank uses to control the money supply.

Because the Federal Reserve Banks control the amount of borrowing, they are able to warn banks who borrow too much or too often or for too long of a time. The Federal Reserve Bank usually does not want to refuse borrowing, but they will let it be known to the member bank that they are over welcoming their borrowing privilege.

The Federal Reserve Banks issue Federal Reserve notes, which are liabilities of the Federal Reserve Bank. The Federal Reserve notes are legal tender for all debts and tax payments. As another method of controlling the money supply, the Federal Reserve Bank can add notes into circulation by buying U.S. government securities or pay notes out to member banks when making loans. The Federal Reserve can also reduce the money supply by selling U.S. government securities and taking in notes.

The ability for the Federal Reserve to add to or reduce the money supply solved a major problem with currency in circulation that had arisen under the national banking system. Remember, earlier we discussed that before the Federal Reserve system, in the fall, when business usually expands and banks have to pay out a great deal of currency, they would find themselves short of money. Member banks now have the ability to obtain additional currency from the Federal Reserve Banks as needed to meet the demand during peak periods. After the first of the year, bank customers usually deposit more currency than they take out. The member banks can then return the excess currency to the Federal Reserve Banks. The result is that the seasonal shortage of currency that was a major problem in the national banking system has been eliminated.

Until 1933, Federal Reserve notes were liabilities of the Federal Reserve Bank issuing them and were a promise to pay "lawful money" either in gold coin or Treasury currency on demand. They were also known as "demand notes." The only difference between Federal Reserve notes and the private bank notes of the pre-Civil War period was that Federal Reserve notes were "legal tender for all debts public and private," which meant that anyone who offers to pay his debts or taxes in Federal Reserve notes has discharged his obligation. Because the volume of the notes in circulation was large, the legal tender status of Federal Reserve notes ensured that they were accepted in all kinds of transactions. After 1933, the Federal Reserve Banks were no longer obligated to pay out gold coin in exchange for their notes and therefore they were no longer demand notes. But, because of their legal tender status and the fact that everyone was used to exchanging them, they were ensured to be continually accepted as notes for transactions.

The Federal Reserve Banks have the ability to control the volume of bank reserves and money supply at will. When the Federal Reserve makes purchases or sales of U.S. securities it is called "open market operations." The Federal Reserve System can and frequently does use its powers to buy and sell securities to keep the bank reserves constant by selling securities to reduce increases in currency in circulation and buying securities to increase reduction in currency in circulation. The ability to control bank reserves by the use of open market operations is one of the Federal Reserve System's most important powers.

By controlling the money supply, the Federal Reserve System has a strong influence to control economic activity. In recessions, to encourage investment expenditures, the Federal Reserve System will attempt to increase money supply to help increase aggregate income and expenditures by lowering the discount rate, buying securities in the open market, or lowering reserve requirements for banks to encourage loans. In boom times when inflation threatens the economy, the Federal Reserve System may act just the opposite and to keep growth of income and expenditures down they may raise the discount rate, sell securities in the open market, or raise reserve requirements for banks, which would reduce availability for making loans.

In summary, the Federal Reserve System can take action to increase or reduce the discount rates, buy or sell securities in the open market, or reduce or increase reserve requirements to control the money supply.

In 1933, the Federal Reserve was subordinated to the executive branch. It remained there until 1951, when the Federal Reserve and the Treasury department signed an accord granting the Federal Reserve full independence over monetary matters while leaving fiscal matters to the Treasury.

Since 1951, the Federal Reserve has frequently changed focus and adopted different policy approaches as it deemed required by economic cycle and circumstances.

I was entering my first year at Syracuse University and quickly became aware of Paul Volker after he was named and sworn in by President Carter as chairman of the Board of Governors of the Federal Reserve System on August 6, 1979, the month before I entered college. At that time inflation was running rampant and the United States was experiencing bad times from stagflation to inflation. During those years, protests were aimed at the Chairman and the Federal Reserve because Paul Volker did something very bold. He took interest rates up by using the authority of the Federal Reserve's powers and raised the fed funds rate from an average of 11.2 percent in 1979 to a peak at 20 percent by June of 1981.

The fed funds rate is the interest rate set as a target by the Federal Reserve's Federal Open Market Committee for banks that have excess funds or capital deposited in the Federal Reserve Bank to charge other banks that are short of funds that need to be on deposit at the Federal Reserve Bank, usually for overnight as reserve requirements. By changing the target rate, the Federal Reserve can influence the money supply or amount of money in circulation in the U.S. economy. By raising the fed funds rate, money in circulation is reduced, as a result slowing down the rate of inflation. In other words, inflation can rise if there is too much currency in circulation, and the Federal Reserve can influence this by reducing circulation with higher rates.

This Federal Reserve method of controlling inflation may be good to slow down inflation but is not so good for companies in industries that need to borrow money, as the fed funds rate also influences all other major interest rates in the economy. The changes implemented under Paul Volker contributed to a significant recession in the United States in the early 1980s. This caused the highest unemployment levels seen since the Great Depression.

Paul Volker and the Federal Reserve System were under political attack and countrywide protests due to the results of high interest rate costs for industries including construction and farming that needed to borrow money on a seasonal basis. At that time, the critical voices were attacking his policies as hurting the financial future of the nation's economy. Little did they know that by cutting off inflation as quickly and abruptly as he could, he actually helped stabilize the economy for decades to come. In my opinion, Paul Volker took the high road, and at the risk of any further career as the chairman, knew what needed to be done to correct the imbalances in the economy. I would think that most of us are far better off today due to the bold actions of Paul Volker.

For decades, young brokers working in the pits would gather around the Reuters machines on Thursday afternoons to see the weekly release of the money supply numbers. This helped them get an indication of how Friday would be setting up, based on the action of the long bond reacting to the money supply figures. Everyone knew that Paul Volker was watching the money supply figures and that those Thursday afternoon numbers would influence Fed policy, which Volker could change at any time because it didn't require an official Federal Reserve Bank Open Market Committee meeting. Historically, policy decisions are normally released immediately after the Federal Reserve Bank Open Market Committee meets.

Paul Volker was a real get-it-done type of guy who influenced many, in good and bad ways, as the chairman of the Federal Reserve when he was appointed in 1979. He had an agenda and it worked. Volker was reappointed by President Reagan in 1983 and completed his term in 1987.

In August 1987, President Ronald Reagan appointed Alan Greenspan as chairman of the Federal Reserve and he was reappointed by successive presidents every four years until he retired on January 31, 2006.

In October 1987, two months after Greenspan's confirmation, he was challenged by the 1987 stock market crash. He was seen as being effective in controlling the damaging situation when he affirmed that the Federal Reserve was ready to serve as a source of liquidity to support the financial system. I praise his actions, as at the time I felt the leadership that he exerted during and after the crash as a broker on Wall Street.

During his tenure as the chairman of the Federal Reserve, the United States journeyed through unprecedented economic growth, budget surpluses, and a profitable stock market.

Greenspan's handling of the failed Long-Term Capital Management, a highly leveraged hedge fund that was capable of crippling the banking system in 1998, showed leadership similar to that of J. P. Morgan, who back in the Bankers' Panic of 1907 brought together leading financiers and banks to bail out the panic situation. Alan Greenspan himself called upon the major banks and investment banks to help ease the financial pressures of the moment. This particular financial market decline was a panic of the markets, not an economic panic such as a recession. His quickly orchestrated leadership got the financial markets back into equilibrium and liquidity returned to keep the markets moving. In my opinion, he did a wonderful job. Again, I was a broker and understood his involvement and countless sleepless hours he went through to get us back to normal operations.

In 2001, when 9/11 shook the United States both emotionally and financially, Alan Greenspan again stepped up to the plate and swung with the immediate lowering of interest rates to make sure that there was liquidity in the financial system. The country was in a panic, not from a financial mess or recession but from an attack by a foreign philosophy that threatened the existence of the financial system. As time went by and the markets continued to move lower, Greenspan followed by keeping the interest rates low.

Low interest rates, justified by a very low inflationary environment after 2001, was the policy of the Federal Reserve. This policy continued for several years and I remember Greenspan encouraging people to go out and buy homes. Greenspan through his years of study had concluded that the backbone of an economy is its housing sector, and I agree. Almost every business is tied to the housing industry in some way or another and Greenspan encouraged borrowing to purchase homes. I don't believe that he meant to purchase homes for speculation; I believe he felt that people should be able to buy the home they live in as an investment as well as a homestead. Because short-term rates were very low, variable mortgage rates became increasingly popular. There were mortgages that were tied to the three-month, six-month, one-year, or up to five-year U.S Treasury notes. These particularly low rates were attractive to average borrowers who were either told or thought that short-term interest rates would stay low for many years to come and that they didn't need to worry about them going up. Greenspan's plan after 9/11 was to keep interest rates low until he determined that the economy was fully able to operate in a higher interest rate environment after the emotional and psychological attack of 9/11.

As Alan Greenspan and the Federal Reserve kept interest rates low, the American public was running to purchase their dream homes. Mortgages were given to people who would not normally qualify through "no income verification loans," which meant as long as the house had value, it could be used as collateral in case the borrower(s) defaulted on their mortgages. Simply, the bank would sell the house to recoup their loan. These were called subprime mortgages.

In 2003, Greenspan began to increase short-term rates from their artificially low levels as the economy showed signs of stabilizing. The mortgage lending business was in full force, signing up everyone they could to get low interest rate variable mortgages. In 2005 and 2006, the variable mortgages that were written in the prior years based on short-term rates began to climb in their monthly payments. The people who took out these mortgages began to realize that their payments were increasing at a faster rate than their incomes. In a September 16, 2007 interview on *60 Minutes* after he left as chairman of the Federal Reserve, Greenspan admitted that, "While I was aware a lot of these practices were going on, I had no notion of how significant they had become until very late. I didn't really get it until very late in 2005 and 2006." In other words, he missed the significance of the subprime mortgages, which I say had a big effect on the housing industry and the economy as a whole. Some economists claim that he created the problem by keeping interest rates too low for too long of time.

I believe that Greenspan, as the chairman of the Federal Reserve, should had known something was amiss, as millions of Americans were buying homes who would not have qualified for the mortgage if it was at a higher fixed rate instead of a low variable rate that one day would inevitably go up. Also, he should have realized that the prices of real estate were climbing at unsustainable levels. Greenspan, earlier on in the late 1990s, was able to let us know that he believed the stock market valuations were getting a little too high. I don't understand how he missed the housing bubble.

But, in Greenspan's defense, let me say that it was not directly his fault. The missed oversight of the whole mortgage industry is to blame. Congressional leaders were encouraging institutions to write as many mortgages as possible, especially in the subprime levels. I'm not sure of the exact reason but I could probably guess that it was political, as some politicians were looking for support for their campaigns to keep their jobs and careers going. Unfortunately for us, these same politicians who encouraged the writing of mortgages are still in power today and are looking like heroes trying to solve the very problem they themselves helped create. They have gone as far as to blame the system or Greenspan or even the whole Federal Reserve for the mess.

The true reality didn't come to light until Alan Greenspan retired as chairman of the Federal Reserve. On February 1, 2006, Ben Bernanke succeeded Alan Greenspan as the new chairman of the Federal Reserve. Bernanke inherited the housing problem that was brewing for several years. Unfortunately, Bernanke was in the academic field prior to becoming chairman, as the chair of the department of economics at Princeton University. Bernanke has been described as a student of the Great Depression, which he has studied in great detail.

As chairman Bernanke's term was starting, the heat of the subprime mortgage meltdown was beginning to appear. Several economists and Wall Street leaders had a good sense of what was coming toward the American economy with such force that they spoke openly about the situation. Publicly and privately, calls were made to the Federal Reserve to lower short-term interest rates in order to keep the variable subprime mortgages from experiencing increased interest rates and monthly payments.

Bernanke held rates steady and the calls were ignored until it finally started. Mortgages started to default in large quantities. A bigger problem was that the mortgages were held by different owners throughout the globe. As packaged products, pension plans and institutions held some form of subprime mortgages in their respective portfolios. It even went so far as investment by money market funds, which eventually "broke the buck" as the mortgages became worth less than their original value or became worthless as the property values backing them began to decrease at a rapid rate. The markets went into a panic as write-downs of the losses being incurred were even at banks' reserve levels. The system began to freeze as word got out that the subprime loans buried in all different financial sectors of the world were becoming worthless.

Then, the panic began. Loans and availability of credit lines were being cut day after day. In essence, I would say that the whole world had a margin call, which meant that no one wanted outstanding debt and lenders wanted to be repaid or discontinue offering loans. The banking system was in the process of a complete meltdown and was locked for credit. The results were dramatic. Bear Stearns, a large player in the subprime industry, was an orchestrated forced buyout by the Federal Reserve to J. P. Morgan Chase Bank. Merrill Lynch was a forced marriage to Bank of America, and Lehman Brothers, holding out for their bailout by the Federal Reserve, never made it, as the bailout never materialized. Lehman Brothers filed bankruptcy.

Furthermore, AIG, the insurance giant, had insured financial instruments such that if they became worthless, then AIG would pay out on the loss. Two things happened here: (1) AIG had too many losses to cover based on their current capital, and (2) some of their investments were in subprime mortgages and became nonliquid. At some point, it was determined that AIG was too big to fail. It was perceived, at the time, that AIG had to stay in business and pay the insurance to its policy owners or these owners, who were other institutions, would fail, creating a chain reaction not only in the United States but all over the world.

Here is where the problem lies as I ask these questions. Who chose which firms were going to merge and why? Why was it so important to a few institutions that AIG survive? Why did the Federal Reserve allow Lehman Brothers to go out of business?

Furthermore, the Federal Reserve made some of these buyout deals occur as it incurred bad assets on its balance sheet and allowed the acquiring companies to not have much skin in the game. Today, the balance sheet of the Federal Reserve must look kind of scary. As this credit facility has taken in bad debt in exchange for dollars to keep the system liquid, the assets being held by the Federal Reserve are in question as to even having any value. I guess time will tell.

And to make matters worse, the U.S. government is now the owner or majority owner of AIG, the new General Motors, and Citibank.

Bernanke, who I believe panicked himself, has lowered interest rates to 0.25 percent and as of this writing intends to keep rates low for an extended period of time. As he is a student of the Great Depression, one of his beliefs is that the Great Depression took place because of tightening of the money supply by the Federal Reserve. So in order to keep the system flowing, he has flooded the money supply with dollars using the powers of the Federal Reserve.

Leading the United States into the Next Cycle

In my opinion, Bernanke knows that it is too late to stop the next Great Depression that's in its early stages. And even though there may be a few similarities and comparisons to the Great Depression, the housing meltdown and deteriorating corporate profits are far worse today than in the Great Depression. If people don't spend money and start the long-term savings process similar to what has been happening in Japan for over 19 years then we can expect negative to zero growth in our economy for many years to come. Bernanke has expanded the balance sheet of the Federal Reserve to extreme levels, dropped interest rates to basically zero, and has flooded the economy with dollars. But these policies have not replaced the trillions of dollars lost in financial and real estate assets, and the worst is yet to come based on historical cycles of deflation. Bernanke has dropped the ball early in his chairmanship of the Federal Reserve. We will now be faced with a further declining stock market, high unemployment for many years to come, and a deflationary environment where the longer you hold on to dollars, the stronger the buying power they will have.

Furthermore, based on actions in the last few years such as bailouts and forced mergers, I believe many people agree that too many strange and secret activities have taken place through the Federal Reserve banking system. I also suggest that the Federal Reserve should not be in existence in its current form by 2013, around the time of its 100-year anniversary.

Today, the Federal Reserve's mandate is to conduct monetary policy to pursue maximum employment, stable prices, and moderate long-term interest rates. It adjusts credit conditions within the economy to achieve this goal. The problem is that they can never get it exactly right. The economy is a constantly moving target with trillions of transactions taking place every day. There are many different cycles that play a major role in our economy and the U.S. government has left it to the Federal Reserve to determine which cycle and which indicator they are going to focus on at any given time. This is why economies, not just the United States, go through boom and bust periods. We recently had our boom period similar to the Roaring Twenties in the United States. In my opinion, we are about to enter the bust period. Credit expansion was so big and out of control up until 2007 that as we enter into a credit dismantling environment the Federal Reserve will not have the power to stop the deflationary cycle. The Federal Reserve has dropped interest rates to basically zero. But on top of that they have, with the help of the U.S. Treasury, decided to bail out bankrupt banks, highly leveraged brokerage firms, poorly managed insurance companies, and manufacturing companies as they were deemed important for the safety of the economy.

The Federal Reserve has also purchased bad assets off the balance sheets of financial institutions and is keeping them on their own balance sheet, hoping that one day in the future they will become viable assets again. Between the Federal Reserve and the U.S. Treasury, there have been programs designed to increase lending and promote consumer spending when consumers already are having difficulty paying their current debt. Their answer is to put the consumer into more debt to help spur consumer spending to save the system. They are doing everything in their power to try to save the system that is entering into a natural deleveraging cycle.

The main culprit is that consumers have lost confidence in the economic policies. They are more concerned today about their own financial security, and money can't buy confidence in this cycle. The only thing that can stop the coming deflationary depression is time. Similar to what has happened in Japan since 1990, bailouts, low interest rates, and the pumping of money into the system cannot convince public opinion that these policies work and the future is solved. It will take many years to regain the trust and confidence of the consumer, and the Federal Reserve just needs to wait it out like a fever and let it burn its way through the economy until prosperity can begin to develop again as in the past. Boy, does history keep repeating itself.

Actions by the centralized banks have come into question since the first government-incorporated national bank, Bank of North America, began in 1782. Many have come and gone due to questionable activities. Today, there are a lot of questions surrounding activities of the current Federal Reserve Banking System and accordingly its days could be numbered. The current system since 1914, when it was created, did not prevent the 1929 stock market crash, the 1937– 1938 stock market decline, the 1973–1974 stock market decline, the October 19, 1987 Black Monday selloff in the stock market, the October 13, 1989 Friday the thirteenth mini crash in the stock market, the September 16, 1992 Black Wednesday selloff in the stock market, the October 27, 1997 mini crash in the stock market, the March 10, 2000 beginning of the dot.com bubble bursting, the stock market downturn of 2002, and the current U.S. bear market that began in 2007.

The secrecy of recent Federal Reserve Bank activities has come into question by Congressman Ron Paul from Texas and Congressman Alan Grayson from Florida, both in the House of Representatives. Recently they introduced an amendment based on HR 1207 which is also known as the Paul-Grayson "Audit the Fed" amendment. The amendment was passed by the House Financial Services Committee by a 43–26 vote on November 19, 2009.

According to the Paul-Grayson Amendment, the new legislation will:

- Remove the blanket restrictions on Government Accountability Office (GAO) audits of the Federal Reserve.
- Allow an audit of every item on the Federal Reserve's balance sheet, all credit facilities, all securities purchase programs, and so forth.
- Retain limited audit exemption on unreleased transcripts and minutes.
- Set a 180-day time lag before details of the Federal Reserve's market actions may be released.

More importantly, it also states that nothing in the amendment shall be construed as interference in or dictation of monetary policy by Congress or the Government Accountability Office (GAO).

"While HR 3996, if passed, will grant sweeping new powers to the Federal Reserve at least with this amendment attached, it won't be acting in secret anymore. This is a major victory for Federal Reserve transparency and government accountability," stated Congressman Paul in his press release immediately after its passage.

Who Owns the Federal Reserve?

According to the Federal Reserve, the Federal Reserve Bank is an independent entity within the government.

The Federal Reserve obtains its authority from the U.S. Congress and is considered to be independent because its decisions do not have to be ratified by the president or anyone else in the executive or legislative branch of government. It also claims that it does not receive funding appropriated by Congress.

The Federal Reserve is subject to oversight by Congress through periodic reviews of its activities and decisions. Congress can change the responsibilities of the Federal Reserve by statute. The Federal Reserve must work within the framework of the overall objectives of economic and financial policy established by the government. As the Federal Reserve describes it, they are "independent within the government."

But the 12 regional Federal Reserve Banks are organized like private corporations. The district Reserve Banks issue shares of stock to banks who are members of the Federal Reserve System. The Reserve Banks accordingly are not operated for profit. By law, member banks must own a certain amount of stock as a condition of membership in the system. The stock is not allowed to be sold, traded, or pledged as security for a loan by a member bank. Also, by law, the member bank receives a six percent dividend per year.

Chapter 9

Famous Market Manias

All types of markets move higher and lower based on some force or belief of investors. Throughout history, markets have behaved by roaring higher with no bottom in sight or selling off sharply as if it was the end of time. These are market manias. When investors turn into speculators or take action when they hear how everyone else is making money, as we recently experienced in the dot.com period of the late 1990s, fortunes can be made and lost. The mania of prices moving to such extreme levels over periods of time is what I call the herd effect. Many get caught up in the herd and are convinced that the longer they wait the more they will miss those great profit opportunities that their friends have been making. It is very difficult for the average investor to understand when he or she is in the middle of a mania. The mania basically dislodges prices, which inaccurately reflects the fundamental economic environment.

The main difference between a market mania and a bull market is the relative economics behind a market move. For instance, in the current environment, the stock market has been in a constant uptrend, moving higher since March 2009, where the fundamentals don't match the expected growth of the price to earnings ratios of most stocks. Also, estimated gross national product growth projected by some analysts has been recently based on stock prices, not economic fundamentals. It's like the analysts don't want to be left behind. The higher the market goes, so do the estimates. The analysts have been adjusting their models as if the stock market is correct. The overextended market seems to be pricing in extreme rapid growth that has not been seen for decades. At the same time, the overvalued expectations would be difficult to meet with the high levels of unemployment and less demand for credit we are experiencing today. The current market reminds me of the NASDAQ Composite market bubble which peaked in 2000 and still has not recovered. A mania also has the characteristic of a parabolic move. In other words, the market grinds higher and higher, which does not give the investor who missed the advance to enter on a pullback. Then, all of a sudden, one day the buyers all become sellers and the mania ends—the bubble pops!

In this chapter, we will discuss seven famous market manias: the Tulip Bulb Mania (1634–1637), the South Sea Bubble (1719–1722), the Dow Jones Industrial Average (1921–1932), the Value Line Composite Index (1965–1975), the Gold Market (1975–2000), the Nikkei 225 Index (1985–2009?) and the Dow Jones Industrial Average again (1980–2009?). We can learn from history that manias and bubbles continue to occur. Natural human behavior, along with market cycles, continues in history to trace out manias that seem too good to be true. It is important to review previous market manias to remind us that we could be in the middle of one now and help us detect them. Our current economic storm was created by a housing mania that resulted in a major stock market pullback. I will discuss how to profit in these manias and bubbles at the end of the chapter. In the meantime, I suggest you observe the structure of the manias.

The Tulip Bulb Mania (1634–1637)

A very famous story about a mania in the seventeenth century takes place in the Netherlands. The Gouda Tulip Bulb Mania has been widely used as a great example of what a mania can act like.

The tulip was an imported luxury originating from Turkey. It could be transplanted easily and could be reproduced by separating the outgrowths. One variety in particular, the Gouda bulb, became

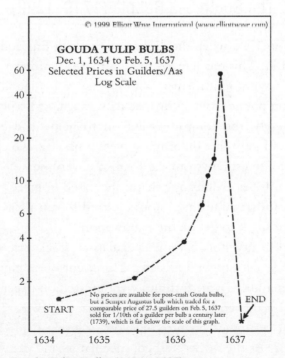

Figure 9.1   Gouda Tulip Bulbs (1634–1637)
SOURCE: Courtesy of Elliott Wave International. Reprinted with permission.

prized for its red and yellow blooms. As demand for the Gouda bulb increased, so did the price. Speculators would buy the Gouda bulbs out of season to sell them to the planters when they were in demand. Speculation became so outrageous that buyers were not only buying for the current planting season, but were now speculating on buying seasons that were years away. Overspeculation caused the Gouda tulip bulb's price to explode as many took most of their savings or borrowed money to get into the craze of owning the Gouda bulb for future delivery.

Unfortunately, three years later in 1637 the bottom fell out and it was disastrous. As shown in Figure 9.1, the price of the Gouda bulbs came crashing down, leaving many speculators with lost savings and close to worthless investments in the bulbs.

The South Sea Bubble (1719–1722)

It all began in 1720 when the House of Lords in England passed the South Sea Bill. This bill allowed the South Sea Company, a monopoly, to trade with South America in exchange for lending England seven million pounds to help finance its war against France.

Accordingly, the company went on to help finance the thirty million pound debt that the English were amassing, which carried a five percent interest rate from the English government.

The South Sea Company's shares increased in price by 10 times their value. Other companies' stocks started to run up as new companies issued stock to get on the bandwagon.

As English investors became speculators, stock prices increased at a rapid rate with no end in sight. This went on in almost all sectors of the market as large fortunes were created on paper.

Then, by the end of 1720, the mania was over. The bubble burst and prices came down to their lowest levels in 1722, as shown in Figure 9.2. As the stocks crashed, speculators and passive investors lost quite a bit of money. Many became destitute overnight. The

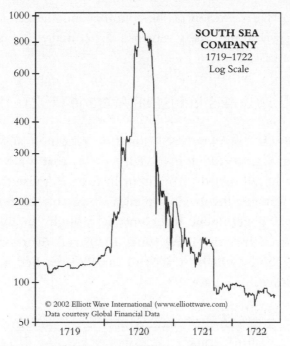

Figure 9.2   South Sea Company (1719–1722)
SOURCE: Courtesy of Elliott Wave International. Reprinted with permission.

whole country experienced a great loss of money and property. It has even been written that suicides became a daily occurrence.

Many who lost their savings were looking for revenge. The post-master general had committed suicide by taking poison. The South Sea Company directors were arrested and lost all their assets. Members of the House of Commons and employees of the South Sea Company were blamed for the crash. Bankers were angry as they, too, lost money at the end of the bubble.

A proponent of the South Sea Company from the start, Robert Walpole, took control and sorted out the country's economy. After he was made Chancellor of Exchequer, he went on to divide the national debt that was all in the South Sea Company into the Bank of England, the Treasury, and a sinking fund. The sinking fund was designed to take a portion of the country's income and put it aside every year, which ultimately returned the country to a more stable financial status.

The Dow Jones Industrial Average (1921–1932)

In 1920, there was a severe economic recession and the U.S. government wasn't getting involved, a policy that is always a good idea, as we have learned throughout history. Because the government did not get involved, capitalism was able to flourish and that lack of government intervention brought in the Roaring Twenties. In 1921, the Dow Jones Industrial Average began its eight-year climb, which by its end in 1929 reached a climax or mania as shown in Figure 9.3.

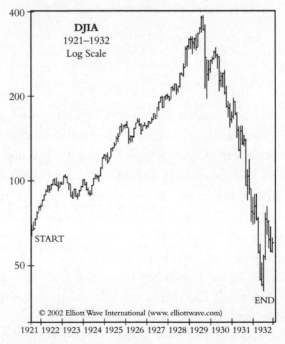

Figure 9.3 Dow Jones Industrial Average (1921–1932)
SOURCE: Courtesy of Elliott Wave International. Reprinted with permission.

Fortunes were made as stocks were climbing without a healthy pullback. Money was flowing as people were enjoying life and its riches. The stock market became the talk of the town as to how to make easy and fast money.

Stocks were moving with such a climb that even those who had never invested before jumped in. Speculators were pushing stocks to way beyond historical valuations based on earnings and dividends.

But in 1929, the bubble burst. It took only one day for investors, speculators, and traders to decide to sell their holdings all at the same time. As the tape kept rolling, sellers kept on selling. Finally, in 1930, a short-term bottom was found and stocks rebounded some 50 percent. But policies of the new and infant Federal Reserve did not bode well for the rally and stocks continued their slide for two more years until the market ran out of sellers.

The final results of the government and the Federal Reserve policies to save the economy and the stock market led to the beginning of the Great Depression. If only the government and the Federal Reserve had stepped back and let natural market forces evolve as they did in 1920, then the economy most likely would have adjusted back more quickly and the Great Depression may have been avoided.

The government's involvement in the current financial crisis will likely prolong a recovery for many years to come, much as it did in the aftermath of the Great Depression.

The Value Line Composite Index (1965–1975)

The Value Line Composite Index is a broader look at the stock market as an index versus the most common indexes such as the Dow Jones Industrial Average or the S&P 500 Index. But here, too, a mania developed with the stocks that made up the Value Line Composite Index a few years prior to 1965.

By 1965, money started pouring into the stocks that were in the index as followers of the Value Line philosophy began to use this index as a barometer of the economy. By the time the mania peaked in 1968, the index was up over 80 percent in only three years.

The bubble only began to burst in 1970. The low at that time for the index reached below where the bubble had started in 1965. But that was not a deterrent for buyers as they came back in 1972 for more and pushed the stocks that compose the Value Line Composite Index into a rally that took the index back up to around a 50 percent retracement from its peak in 1968 to the low that was made back in 1970.

As shown in Figure 9.4, the end of the mania finally arrived at extremely low levels in late 1974 as the Value Line Composite Index lost over 70 percent of its value from its peak in 1968. This is a great example of a mania turned bubble and then bear market. This cycle took about 10 years to complete.

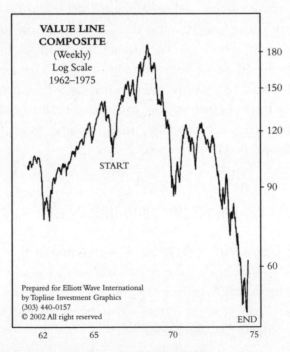

Figure 9.4   Value Line Composite (1962–1975)
SOURCE: Courtesy of Elliott Wave International. Reprinted with permission.

The Spot Gold Bubble (1975–2000)

Gold has had a strong presence in the history of investing and is either observed as a safe haven when there is instability in the world or used as a hedge against inflation as it retains its value. But a mania occurred in the gold market in 1980 as its price soared to over $800 an ounce in a very short period of time.

As the stock markets were coming out of their 1973 and 1974 low periods, gold reached a low below $100 an ounce in 1976. Over the next several years, the price of gold began to climb in what looked like an orderly fashion until the mania broke loose.

Speculators and investors could not get enough of the precious metal going into 1980 as the price soared from around $400 an ounce to over $800 an ounce in two months as shown in Figure 9.5. This mania was pushed by speculative buying and the fear of inflation.

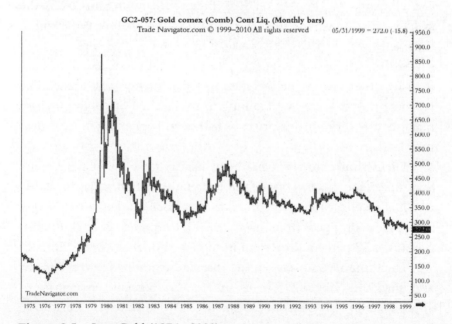

Figure 9.5   Spot Gold (1976–2000)
SOURCE: Genesis Financial Technologies, Inc. Reprinted with permission.
Prepared by Shaffer Asset Management, Inc. Copyrighted 2009 by Genesis Financial Technologies, Inc.

The gold mania quickly corrected in April and May of 1980 as it fell to under $500 an ounce. At that level, the second wave of buyers tried to push gold higher to just shy of $750 an ounce in September of that same year.

By mid-1982, the mania and speculation died down as gold was not as attractive as it once was. From its peak in 1980 to a low in 1982, gold lost over 65 percent of its value.

All through the rest of the 80s and the 90s, as paper assets such as stocks became the next mania, gold finally made a low in 1999 to below $270 an ounce.

The Nikkei 225 Index (1985–2009?)

Think manias can't happen in the U.S. markets? Let's examine the historical mania of the Nikkei 225 Index. Beginning in 1985, the Nikkei 225 Index was trading at around 10,400. From 1985 until the mania peak in 1990, the Nikkei 225 rallied 375 percent.

Such a strong and sustained speculative rally was also accompanied by other asset value increases in Japan such as real estate. The Japanese people were even coming to the United States to purchase real estate at very inflated prices as had been happening in their own mainland.

Then, similar to what has been occurring here in the United States over the past few years, the real estate market in Japan started to fall. The effect rolled into the Japanese stock market as the Nikkei 225 Index dropped from over 38,000 to under 28,000 in four months, a 27 percent drop from its high as shown in Figure 9.6.

Then, the second wave of late speculators jumped into the mania and lifted the Nikkei 225 Index up for a 50 percent retracement to approximately 33,000 from the January 1990 peak to the April 1990 low. From that level, the Nikkei 225 has continued its descent to a low in 2003 of below 7,700. That equates to a 13-year decline of 79 percent.

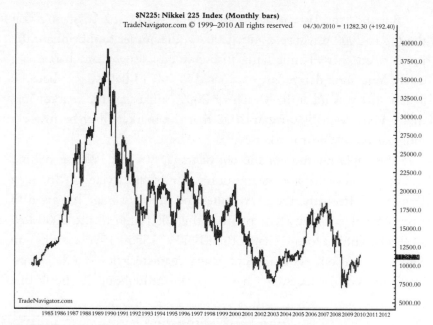

Figure 9.6   The Nikkei 225 Index (1985–2009?)
SOURCE: Genesis Financial Technologies, Inc. Reprinted with permission.
Prepared by Shaffer Asset Management, Inc. Copyrighted 2009 by Genesis Financial
Technologies, Inc.

The Nikkei, after having a several-year rally that peaked at over
17,000 in 2007 as the U.S. markets were near their respective highs,
moved once again below the 10,000 level, making a new low for
the ending of a mania bubble below 7,000.

The aftermath of the Nikkei 225 market mania from 1990 is still
being felt today, as the index is still 70 percent below its all-time high.

The Dow Again (1980–2009?)

Finally, let's take another look at the Dow Jones Industrial Average.
Between 1980 and 1982, the Dow Jones Industrial Average was in
the beginning stages of a major market mania that would last until
2000. There were some minor corrections along the way, such as in
1987 and 1994, to adjust for overspeculation.

But the long lasting mania of buying stocks was so strong that the top in 2000 was surpassed in 2007 with another top, bringing the index to another all-time high. I observe on a long-term chart that a classic long-term delayed top occurred in 2007. I believe that because a new low was made in March of 2009, surpassing the market low that was made in November 2002 that the markets may be in for a long period of a bear market cycle.

The euphoria and excitement of the 1980s and 1990s is behind us and I believe we are on the other side of that cycle as shown in Figure 9.7. Recently, the Dow Jones Industrial Average has risen to over a 50 percent retracement from the 2007 high to the 2009 low in similar fashion to the chart of the Nikkei 255 in 1990 as shown in Figure 9.6. As our economy enters the characteristics of a deflationary depression I expect, as I have written throughout this book that

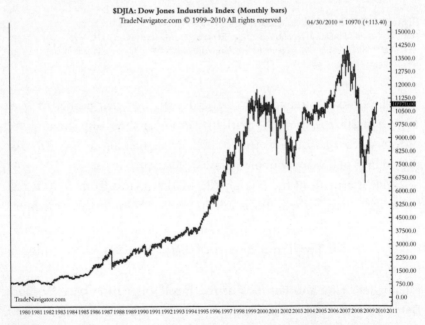

Figure 9.7   The Dow Jones Industrial Average Again (1980–2009?)
SOURCE: Genesis Financial Technologies, Inc. Reprinted with permission.
Prepared by Shaffer Asset Management, Inc. Copyrighted 2009 by Genesis Financial Technologies, Inc.

the Dow Jones Industrials will continue to move lower as consumer prices deflate and credit becomes less available.

Detecting the Next Market Mania

Detecting the next mania or bubble is not an easy task. Over the years, just as traders today sell rallies and buy weakness, investors who were able to take a longer term view than just the day, week, or even month were able to visualize a mania or bubble from many environmental factors. Some of the clues include the media. By the time the story of how prices are going higher hits the mainstream media on covers of magazines, headlines in the newspapers, or nightly news, that should be your first signal that the frenzy may be near its end. As I mentioned in earlier chapters, the herd effect can take prices to unreasonable levels. Another clue is similar to what we are currently experiencing with price action in the stock market and the gold market. As prices begin to move in a parabolic structure, with no healthy pullbacks or corrective down waves, investors who missed the earlier price action begin to jump in, pushing prices unreasonably higher. Another clue of a mania or bubble is the time frame. Healthy markets don't particularly move up fast and within short periods of time. Take a step back and review the time factor and percentage returns. If these seem unrealistic or too good to be true, then I believe that you are observing a mania or bubble in the market.

The goal here is not to try to make a profit on the entire move in prices. The objective would be to realize a mania or bubble is taking place by the price action and jump in and out quickly so as not to get caught when the mania begins to subside or the bubble bursts. Today, I speak with many traders and investors who have profited handsomely because of their recognition that many markets can move rather quickly in one direction or another in a heartbeat. Under the current economic storm, which I believe will be with us for many more years to come, these people jump in and out in order to capture profits. You can do this, too, with discipline.

Develop a plan of time and price with specific objectives. These objectives should be focused on your level of risk. If you believe that we are currently in a mania of stocks increasing too rapidly, have an exit strategy that will either lock in profits from where your position is now or reduce your losses if the market moves against you. Taking losses is part of the strategy of investing. We all experience periods of losses and periods of profits. The goal in every situation, but most certainly during manias or bubbles, is to take money out of the market before it takes it out of you. If the volatility becomes too large for you to handle, sitting out until you see a better, more profitable opportunity would not be a bad idea. One thing to remember is to invest or trade with your head, not over it.

Part Four

NATURE'S ROLE IN ENGINEERING THE MARKETS

Chapter 10

Natural Cycles and the Financial Markets

We've discussed human nature, psychology, the mechanics and history of our financial system, and now we turn our attention to finance theory and the engineering of the markets. While it may seem like an odd turn we're about to make, studying finance theory and the markets can be enriched by studying nature's cycles. In this chapter, we will look at solar cycles, climate change, and our ecosystem as possible indicators of changes in the financial markets and at the very least, good comparisons for learning a lesson about flexibility.

I begin Part Four with natural cycles as they relate to the markets because there is a force, stronger than us, that may control cycles in the markets. We are only the observers, as Albert Einstein so eloquently stated in his writings. There are a few market technicians

141

that actually make market predictions based on the alignment of the sun, moon, and the earth along with the cycles that each one has within itself. It is important to be quite aware that these relationships exist as they could assist you to stay disciplined and profit in economic storms.

Using Solar Cycles as Indicators

In 1610, Galileo Galilei was viewing the sun through his new telescope and saw what appeared to be dark spots on the sun's surface. It was then that he made the first observation of what were to be known as sunspots. Sunspots appear when temperatures in the dark centers are cooler than the surrounding areas and they can last from several days to several months, depending on their size. The size of sunspots can vary enormously. They may be anywhere between a few hundred miles to as much as a quarter of a million miles in diameter. They also often appear in clusters. It is believed that sunspots are intense magnetic forces that exist below the surface of the sun with magnetic field strengths over thousands of times stronger than the Earth's magnetic field. When the magnetic fields change, so do the temperatures, creating cooler areas and the appearance of dark spots.

The magnetic fields change over a period of time, giving rise to a cyclic change in the level of sunspot activity. During a time of minimum activity the magnetic fields run from the sun's north to its south. As the sun rotates the fields rotate at different speeds, with the equatorial regions spinning more slowly than the poles. This causes the fields within the sun to change and eventually align themselves in an east–west direction. At this time there is a peak in sunspot activity. The rotation of the sun continues and the fields gradually revert back to a north–south direction. In this way there is a cyclic change in the level of sunspot activity.

The sunspots usually come in groups with two sets of spots. One set has a positive magnetic field while the other set has a negative magnetic field. The magnetic field is strongest in the darker or cooler parts of the sunspots called the umbra. The magnetic field is weaker in the lighter part called the penumbra.

Continuous daily observations were started at the Zurich Observatory in 1849 and earlier observations were used to put together records dating back to 1610. A simple count of the sunspots that are visible on the surface of the sun at any given time does not give a good assessment of sunspot activity. A scientist named Rudolf Wolf, who was director of the Zurich Observatory shortly after the discovery of sunspots, devised a system to assign a figure for the relative sunspot activity. This figure, known as the sunspot number, is not actually the number of sunspots that can be seen, but a relative figure that provides an indication of the activity.

The formula for counting sunspots was designed to give reliable numbers even during difficult observing conditions, as most sunspot groups have an average number of spots. Monthly averages of the sunspot numbers show that the numbers of sunspots that are visible on the sun increase and diminish with an approximate 11-year cycle. But these cycles can be as short as seven years or as long as 14 years.

There are at least two official sunspot numbers reported. The International Sunspot Number is compiled by the Solar Influences Data Analysis Center in Belgium and the NOAA sunspot number is compiled by the U.S. National Oceanic and Atmosphere Administration.

So what does this mean for us here on Earth? It's important to know about the approximate 11-year cycle, and also the interaction between the sun and the Earth within the sunspot cycles, because they result in a considerable disturbance in the magnetic field. Large levels of electromagnetic energy, including ultraviolet light and X-rays, are released and when they reach the Earth, they ionize the gases in our ionosphere.

When I was a young boy, I was fascinated by the concept of radio and late at night I would enjoy listening to far away stations. It was amazing to me that voices could carry through the air like that. Radio waves, which are propagated by an antenna, are electromagnetic cycles of energy that are commonly known as frequencies. Frequency is the name given due to the frequency of the electromagnetic cycles. One kilocycle is equal to one thousand waves or cycles per second and one megacycle is equal to one million waves or cycles per second. For example, 880 on your AM radio dial means that the electromagnetic waves cycle, or are frequent, by 880 thousand times per second, and it is known as 880 kilocycles. Eventually, credit was give to Heinrich Rudolf Hertz (1857–1894) who was the first to create radio waves artificially. Today, instead of the kilocycle or megacycle, they are known as kilohertz and megahertz. Therefore, 880 kilocycles would be known as 880 kilohertz and would be abbreviated as 880 kHz.

I discovered the power of sunspot cycles when I became an amateur radio operator as a young boy. During certain years, radio bands or frequencies would be "open" for communication all over the world. Then there would be years when it became impossible to even communicate across town on the same frequency and therefore it was classified as "closed" to long distance communication. These open and closed radio bands were a direct result of sunspot cycle activities. In radio, these conditions are called propagation.

Sunspot cycles are accompanied by major flares or plumes of fire that emit off the sun and create strong electromagnetic energies that hit the earth's outer layers. The ionosphere is the layer in the atmosphere around the earth that can be changed by the sun's electromagnetic energy to allow radio frequency transmissions to pass through to the outer space, which results in the radio band being "closed," or be changed to deflect radio frequencies back to bounce around the earth on an angle that would rest far away from where you are located, which results as the band being "open."

For example, during the daylight hours, you will most likely hear local radio stations at the top end of your AM dial. This is the effect of the sun's energy thinning out a particular layer within the ionosphere and allowing radio waves to escape into the atmosphere. But at night, when the sun sets, you will be able to hear stations from hundreds of miles away, because the sun is not directly sending energy to the ionosphere, thereby allowing the ionosphere to thicken and reflect radio waves back to the earth. This results in the waves bouncing from land to the ionosphere and back down again. This phenomenon allows distant transmitted radio signals to reach your radio receiver.

Now, imagine the above example instead occurring not only daily but over an 11-year cycle. High frequencies are also known as shortwave radio frequencies. With shortwave radios, you can receive radio station signals from countries all over the world. But conditions must be favorable, as they are affected by not only the daily sun cycle as explained in the AM radio example, but they must also be favorable in the 11-year sunspot cycle for the upper high-frequency radio bands. When the number of sunspots is high, this condition creates solar flares, which increase emitted radiation from the sun toward the earth's atmosphere, therefore increasing propagation for some of the upper high-frequency bands. It would be as if the ionosphere thickens and becomes a mirror as it reflects the radio wave energy back toward the earth. This occurs because the energy from the solar flares reaching the ionosphere ionizes certain layers in the ionosphere, thereby increasing its ability to reflect radio waves at the upper high-frequency bands back toward the earth. The opposite is also true, that when sunspot levels are low, there are few, if any, solar flares or eruptions that take place on the sun, which causes conditions to decline and closes some of the upper high-frequency bands as the ionosphere is not ionized and radio waves just pass through it into outer space.

NASA Issues a Warning

According to the NASA web site and as of March 31, 2009, sunspot activity has reached a 100-year low dating back to 1913, which has some scientists concerned about the future. "We're experiencing a very deep solar minimum," says solar physicist Dean Pesnell of the Goddard Space Flight Center. "This is the quietest sun we've seen in almost a century," agrees sunspot expert David Hathaway of the Marshall Space Flight Center.

Why is the sun so quiet and without activity? No one can accurately predict the exact timing of the sunspot cycles but some record lows are being made in some of the indicators that are followed closely by scientists. For instance, the sun is at the lowest level of solar wind pressure since such measurements began in the 1960s, a 50-year low. Also, there is a 12-year low in solar irradiance, which is the sun's brightness. Finally, telescopes are recording the dimmest sun since 1955. All of these lows indicate weakness in the sun's global magnetic field.

The concern is that something weird is going on and that the current extreme low in the sunspot cycle, similar to the stock market, can be followed by an unusually high sunspot cycle leading to a solar maximum, or in other words, a peak in sunspot activity.

So the question remains because sunspot cycles are difficult to predict. Will the cycle reach an even further low between 2011 and 2012, tracking the cycle in the stock market, or have we seen the lows in the sunspot activity and are now facing an even stronger-than-usual peak in sunspot activity in 2012? Either way, our analysis is currently indicating a stock market low in the United States in approximately year 2012, which coincides with either a sunspot low or high depending on the cycle. Scientists are predicting a solar maximum of activity in sunspots in 2012 that could be the strongest in modern times.

Could the sun be coiling down to create a huge solar storm? The end of the sunspot lows begins with solar flares that could become violent if the current low is setting up for a major storm. In May 2009, a major sunspot appeared in the backside of the sun and was captured by NASA's equipment. "This is the biggest event we've seen in a year or so," said Michael Kaiser, research scientist with the heliophysics division at NASA Goddard Space Flight

Center. "Does this mean we're finished with the minimum or not? It's hard to say. This could be it. It's got us all excited." Because this sunspot occurred in the typical early locations on the sun, Kaiser is sure this is part of the new cycle.

If a major solar storm does occur, scientists conclude that there will be severe damage to power grids and other communication systems with the potential to reach catastrophic levels. The predictions are based in part on the major solar storm of 1859, also known as the Carrington Event. During that storm, telegraph wires were shorted out, igniting fires in the United States and Europe. Another episode occurred in New York City in May of 1921 where the entire signal and switching system of the New York Central Railroad below 125th Street went down and a fire broke out in the control tower at 57th Street and Park Avenue. Also, in the same 1921 solar storm, a fire destroyed the Central New England railroad station, and in Sweden, a telephone station was burned out and the storm interfered with telephone, telegraph, and cable traffic over most of Europe. Recent episodes took place in 1989 when the sun released a huge solar flare that knocked out power to all of Quebec, Canada. A 1994 solar storm caused major malfunctions to two communications satellites, disrupting newspaper, network television, and nationwide radio service throughout Canada. And in 2003, there was a sequence of 10 major solar flares during a two-week period that knocked out two orbiting satellites and damaged an instrument aboard the Mars orbiter. But a repeat of the 1859 solar storm could cause more extensive social and economic disruptions.

A report by the National Academy of Sciences found that if a storm as severe as one in 1859 occurred today, it could cause $1 to 2 trillion in damage the first year and that it could take four to ten years to recover. "As severe as these recent events have been, the historical record reveals that space weather of even greater severity has occurred in the past and suggests that such extreme events, although rare, are likely to occur again some time in the future," the report states. According to the report, the "vulnerability of modern society and its technological infrastructure to space weather has increased dramatically" over the past century and a half. The report concludes that education, training, and public awareness are a priority to develop preventive actions or plans.

If the details of this report come true, then there will be a definite effect on the economies around the world that I describe as an economic storm. I bring this to your attention for the possibility that this information can be catalyst for a low in the stock market as this study lines up with my other indications of a stock market cycling down for a potential 40-year low. Take note of this cycle and take action if necessary to protect your investments with hedging tools such as exchange-traded funds, index futures, or option protection that all have the ability to be short the market and profit if the market turns lower. Or, take the opportunity to profit from this predicted cycle by just going short. Either way, be forewarned that these cycles exist and take action based on your own analysis and level of risk. There are opportunities to profit from such disturbances and I suggest you be prepared to take advantage of the coming cycle.

Predicting the Stock Market Low

The battle is on for better forecasting abilities before the next peak in solar activity, which is expected to arrive around 2012. Now that the sun has possibly passed a lull, forecasters are acutely aware that solar flares can occur at any moment. Severe space weather is expected to ramp up a year or two before the peak. Finally, some scientists expect the next peak to bring more severe events than other recent peaks.

There are also others who predict the next solar cycle peak can come as late as May of 2013. But it does appear that solar activity has been increasing since September of 2009, and an upward trend may have begun in the solar flux, which has long been used as a barometer of the sun's output.

As far as my prediction and coordination for the next stock market cycle low, if it aligns with the sunspot peak activity, it would be an expected window for the bottom of the stock market cycle between mid-2012 and mid-2013. Furthermore, our current analysis shows that the next bear market deflationary cycle for the stock market low may begin at any time now as the stock market descends. This same period also lines up with the 40-year cycle low which last occurred around the late 1974 period.

Nature's Lessons for Finance

As I've been presenting, there are ways in which nature can predict real and measurable change in the financial markets. The number of sunspots is just one example. But more than serving as an indicator of change, nature can teach us as humans a great deal about how to react to changes in our surroundings, both personally, professionally, and financially. When looking at the financial markets through the prism of nature, there are four lessons we can learn: (1) Change will occur and we need to learn how to cope with it, (2) everything is interconnected (including you), (3) too much regulation of a system can have a negative impact, and (4) choose your advisors wisely. There are a lot of financial gurus willing to tell you which way the market is going to go and when to buy or sell a particular stock. Take a cue from nature on these four points and you'll be one step closer to understanding modern-day finance theory and how markets are engineered.

Change Is Inevitable

It has been noted that very few sunspots were observed from about 1645 to 1715. This inactivity period corresponds to a climatic period known as the Little Ice Age when snow on land and rivers that were normally ice free, froze all year round at lower altitudes. There is also evidence that the sun had similar periods of inactivity in the faraway past. Connection between solar activity and terrestrial climate is an ongoing study.

Since the Little Ice Age, there have been no long droughts in the United States—roughly from 1315 to 1865 when Europe and other areas of the world were experiencing about a one degree cooler temperature. It has also been studied that prior to the Little Ice Age, a Medieval Warm Period also known as the Medieval Climate Anomaly occurred between 800–1300 A.D. During this period, scientists believe that the Earth was warmer than before and the Little Ice Age followed. Scientists also believe that four of the five long American droughts occurred during the Medieval Warm Period of irregular climate. Probability-wise, maybe our chances are closer to four in five of the twenty-first century having a major climate disturbance with some regions experiencing warmer climate than others.

Some researchers claim that global warming is part of the earth's natural cycle, while others claim that human activity is the primary source of change. As climate continues to change, scientists have noticed that sea levels are rising and are now predicting permanent flooding of countries such as the Netherlands, Bangladesh, Tuvalu, and the Maldives. Well known low-lying cities such as Boston, New York, New Orleans, Miami, and London could also flood.

Through history there have been century-long droughts that have been observed through rings on trees. According to history, the Great Plains and the West have often been through century-long droughts. These droughts were more long lasting than the most recent and familiar Dust Bowl of 1932–1938.

Ancient climate records indicated many sudden jumps in temperatures and rainfall amounts that would last for many centuries before reversing back in the opposite direction. The change in direction was sometimes very abrupt.

Other planets are warming, too. Maybe the climate on Earth is changing because of the sun itself. This could be from the sun having its own cycle affecting its own solar system. For example, Pluto, which is the most distant planet from the sun, has increased in temperature about 3.5 Fahrenheit degrees over the past two decades. Accordingly, if Pluto has warmed 3.5 Fahrenheit degrees from radiant energy from the sun, then Earth, which is 40 times closer to the sun than Pluto, should have warmed more than 18 Fahrenheit degrees. This is clearly not what the Earth has experienced. Another explanation for Pluto's warming may be from the seasonal effects in its 250-year orbital path around the sun.

Throughout climate history, we can observe that the Earth has its own natural cycles of climate change. The Earth, as a planet, has the ability to adjust itself to solar changes that occur from the sun's own natural cycles that hit the Earth's atmosphere. That's when nature takes its course. Records show that swings in climate change were here long before humans inhabited the Earth. Some even believe that the solar system that the Earth is a part of is still expanding.

Many people do not like change and have trouble coping with it. But the Earth's natural cycles will continue. Volcanoes will continue to erupt as the inside pressures mount and lava flows down, altering the landscape. Earthquakes will continue to occur as the Earth takes a stretch just as humans do. And climate will change in its own cycles from floods to droughts, such as in our most recent experience in the midwestern United States, particularly in Iowa, where major flooding arrived that had not been seen in over 500 years. Humans didn't cause the flooding; nature took its course. Land masses will shift and adjust just as they have been doing since the beginning of the planet. Accept the changes and adjust your habits and lifestyles to them.

The markets have similar natural characteristics of climate change. One might even say that the climate of the market is gloomy for the moment. History has shown that the markets experience their own climate change, and as investors, we need to adjust our thinking to the changes in the market. The buy and hold strategies for shorter periods of time really didn't help us navigate to increase our wealth for the past 10 years ending December 31, 2009 where the S&P 500 Index had its first negative return since its inception in 1957. I remember being at sales meetings where we were told that the S&P 500 Index has never had a negative 10-year return. Well, I guess they need to take that one out of the program. We need to be aware the there are many factors that cause the market to move up and down such as inflation, deflation, world events, or my favorite, public sentiment, just to name a few. Adjust your portfolios accordingly.

Everything Is Interconnected

Ecosystems are dynamic interactions between plants, animals, and microorganisms and their environment working together as a functional unit. Our 100-million-year-old ecosystem will fail if they do not remain in balance. No group can carry more organisms than its food, water, and shelter can accommodate. Food and territory are often balanced by natural phenomena such as fire, disease, and the number of predators.

Humans have affected ecosystems in almost every way conceivable. Every time we walk out in the wilderness or bulldoze land for a new parking lot we are drastically altering an ecosystem. We have disrupted the food chain, the carbon cycle, the nitrogen cycle, and the water cycle. Mining minerals also takes its toll on an ecosystem. We need to do our best to not interfere in these ecosystems and let nature take its course.

Now how does this relate to the markets? First, the markets are very similar to the ecosystem. Stocks, bonds, currencies, commodities, and other forms of investment vehicles are interrelated. Proof came recently when the fallout of the subprime market affected almost every other type of market in the world. As the subprime market began to fall in value, overnight credit began to tighten and at one point freeze to the point of the inability of many corporations and individuals in need to function properly. This led to liquidation of almost all asset classes as margin calls, redemptions from investors, and lending for leveraged funds were completely halted from their sources.

Our world economic participants are interdependent and when an investment or activity that normally functions to keep the financial wheels in motion falls out of balance, it can devastate portfolios for investors, bring companies to their knees in desperate need of financing, and change the lives of people throughout the world. We cannot always predict when such events are going to occur but we do know that they have occurred in the financial markets since the beginning of time and will continue to arrive in the future. Regulations can only do so much to prevent such economic catastrophes as we have recently experienced after the subprime fallout that began in 2007.

Too Much Regulation Can Be Disruptive

The earth is an incredible recycling machine. All the earth's natural elements follow a cycle of origination to destruction and back to origination again.

For example, when an animal or plant dies in the forest or on the plains, they are slowly broken down by worms, bacteria, and fungi. As the animals or plants are in the rotting process, the substances they were made from pass back into the soil. The soil then gets enriched from these substances, new plants spring up, and as nature takes it, the animals will feed on. Then the animals and plants produce waste. This waste is also, like the rotting animal, broken down and absorbed back into the soil.

Now, sometimes the biogeochemical cycle is upset from activities of people. As a result, a large number of animal and plant species become in danger of extinction if the natural cycles are disrupted.

The markets have their own so-called biogeochemical cycle, too. Investments such as stocks, bonds, or other investment vehicles should naturally move higher or lower based on supply and demand by the participants. Understanding this concept is part of capitalism or the free market. Too many regulations in the markets can reduce the natural effects of investment cycles and cause a disruption to the investment cycle of one particular investment, thereby endangering another investment that should have never been affected by the original regulation. This is something that should always be addressed and I have always felt that free market capitalism should be the foremost and natural way for our markets to function.

Because of not enough regulation or too much regulation, the markets will not be able to function in a consistent manner like the biogeochemical cycle. It is therefore my opinion that markets will form bubbles and busts as humans have in the past and will as in the future interfere with the natural movements of the markets.

Take Advice, but Use Your Head

There are three natural forms of water: solid, liquid, and gas. Water constantly cycles through these forms while in the atmosphere forming a water vapor gas or condensed clouds. On the ground, it is in a liquid form called water or more solid as snow or ice, which both also include rain, sleet, hail and any other forms falling out of the atmosphere. The process of water entering the atmosphere is known as the process of evaporation, which when completed forms condensation in the form of clouds. As the atmosphere fills with the condensation, precipitation is the water falling back down to the earth. This cycle then repeats itself over and over again.

The markets have a similar cycle where they rise to heights over specified periods of time, then fall back to lower levels from which they may have begun. These market up and market down cycles are caused by many reasons, which I speculate would be social moods, economic activity, or market manias and panics. We cannot predict the water cycle precisely—where the water will evaporate from and when it will fall from the sky—but many meteorologists make a living predicting such events. This is the same for market analysis where professionals try to predict market highs and lows time after time. It's just slightly different in the markets because it depends on the method of forecasting the analyst uses or what the time frame is for investing. In fact, wouldn't that be great if we had market technicians or predictors on television forecasting the movements in the markets similar to the weatherpersons. I can see it now: "We're now going over to Dan Shaffer to get the five-day forecast for the markets." Unfortunately, market prediction is not an exact science, it's an art in which an investor must decide which analyst and forecaster he or she is most comfortable with. But investors must realize that it is in their head to control their emotions and greed when it comes to money by listening to the gurus.

Living in Tune with the Cycles

I have reviewed three natural cycles, though there are many more in nature that I didn't mention, that I feel are pertinent to explaining that nature creates cycles or recycles, as do stocks, bonds, currencies, and many other types of investments. Many have made a fortune by following the longer term market cycles such as the recent bull market that began in 1982 and ended in the year 2000. Others have followed seasonal cycles, which under normal market circumstances occur in foreseeable patterns. But cycles in the markets come in many different time frames and it is up to you, the investor, to decide which cycle you would have a higher degree of profiting from.

The problem that one must always be aware of is the regulation by authorities who may not really have the knowledge or experience and therefore throw off the natural cycles of the markets. These obstacles can create tremendous volatility during the longer cycle trends and can cause havoc in your portfolio in the short run. Always be aware of your risk tolerance as you choose which cycle to believe in. Finally, I believe living in tune with the cycles, which can be upset very easily, is a major way to participate in the markets, but one must always remember that trees don't grow to the sky and how low can a stock go? Zero.

Your investment strategy should include disruptions by regulators or politicians that purposefully disrupt the natural order of the markets. As such, your awareness of the effect of governmental policies should be foremost in your decision-making process. Decisions thought to be helpful by those involved can be very harmful to your investments and the economy. Policy changes from several years ago have put our current economy and markets into a storm. The markets will not return to normal for a long period of time, which I believe will be when the governments get out of the investment business and do what they were designed to do: govern. They need to let capitalism survive, and until then, there is no major incentive to invest as investors keep wary of governments changing the rules during the game. Uncertainty is not a reason to invest. Therefore, until a clearer, more definitive future of capitalism can be seen, I suggest that you either take a more conservative approach to investing or hedge your risky positions with exchange-traded funds, index futures, or options during this ongoing economic storm.

Chapter 11

Investment Cycles

There is something mathematically inherent in the markets and the universe. The magic of counting and simple math are constantly around us even if we are not conscious of their existence. In this chapter, I will introduce basic mathematical concepts and theories relating to investment cycles and timing factors that continually expose themselves. In particular, keep in mind that there are many who study the order of the universe. I present those with which I seem to correlate the best.

I have always been fascinated by the power of natural occurrences and the order of the universe—as was Einstein, though I am far from his intelligence level—especially when it comes to mathematics, probability, and statistics. Patterns exist as sequences or cycles all around us and sometimes we are not even aware of them. Here are some mathematical examples:

$$1 \times 8 + 1 = 9$$
$$12 \times 8 + 2 = 98$$
$$123 \times 8 + 3 = 987$$
$$1{,}234 \times 8 + 4 = 9{,}876$$
$$12{,}345 \times 8 + 5 = 98{,}765$$
$$123{,}456 \times 8 + 6 = 987{,}654$$
$$1{,}234{,}567 \times 8 + 7 = 9{,}876{,}543$$
$$12{,}345{,}678 \times 8 + 8 = 98{,}765{,}432$$
$$123{,}456{,}789 \times 8 + 9 = 987{,}654{,}321$$
$$1 \times 9 + 2 = 11$$
$$12 \times 9 + 3 = 111$$
$$123 \times 9 + 4 = 1{,}111$$
$$1{,}234 \times 9 + 5 = 11{,}111$$
$$12{,}345 \times 9 + 6 = 111{,}111$$
$$123{,}456 \times 9 + 7 = 1{,}111{,}111$$
$$1{,}234{,}567 \times 9 + 8 = 11{,}111{,}111$$
$$12{,}345{,}678 \times 9 + 9 = 111{,}111{,}111$$
$$123{,}456{,}789 \times 9 + 10 = 1{,}111{,}111{,}111$$

$$9 \times 9 + 7 = 88$$
$$98 \times 9 + 6 = 888$$
$$987 \times 9 + 5 = 8{,}888$$
$$9{,}876 \times 9 + 4 = 88{,}888$$
$$98{,}765 \times 9 + 3 = 888{,}888$$
$$987{,}654 \times 9 + 2 = 8{,}888{,}888$$
$$9{,}876{,}543 \times 9 + 1 = 88{,}888{,}888$$
$$98{,}765{,}432 \times 9 + 0 = 888{,}888{,}888$$

Mathematics can also form symmetry of nature:

$$1 \times 1 = 1$$
$$11 \times 11 = 121$$
$$111 \times 111 = 12{,}321$$
$$1{,}111 \times 1{,}111 = 1{,}234{,}321$$

$$11,111 \times 11,111 = 123,454,321$$
$$111,111 \times 111,111 = 12,345,654,321$$
$$1,111,111 \times 1,111,111 = 1,234,567,654,321$$
$$11,111,111 \times 11,111,111 = 123,456,787,654,321$$
$$111,111,111 \times 111,111,111 = 12,345,678,987,654,321$$

I read in a recent e-mail that if each letter of the alphabet represented a number (on this scale, A is 1 and Z is 26), then the words "hard work" equal 98 and the word "knowledge" equals 96. However, the word "attitude" gets you to 100. Interesting coincidence!

Thus no matter what life throws us, our positive mental attitudes, as shown in the numbers, can greatly improve our ability to profit with our investments and accept that losing money is part of the game. The same concept can be applied to your personal life, too: Keeping positive about yourself and knowing that you can't change the past, but that you can only change the future, can give you great hope and desire to fulfill your lifelong dreams and maximize your abilities to get where you want. This can lead to a more rewarding life! Learn from your past mistakes, because if you don't remember and learn from them, then you are condemned to relive them.

The Delta Phenomenon

In 1999, I discovered the Delta Society International, which was founded in the early 1980s by J. Welles Wilder Jr. (www.deltasociety .com). His purpose was to share his discovered "secret of the perfect orders behind the markets." He calls it the Delta Phenomenon that is the basis for all market movement relative to time.

It all started in 1983 with a phone call from Jim Sloman from Chicago. He invited Welles to visit him as he had discovered something about the markets that he wanted to show him. Jim was a gifted person. In high school, he placed among the top in the country in a national exam given to all senior math students. After high school, he was awarded a National Merit Scholarship to Princeton University where he studied math and physics in special advanced classes.

Jim called his discovery Delta, a Greek letter derived from a word meaning *door*, and in this case, a door to the unknown. As they sat down at the kitchen table at Jim's home, a chart of the past nine months of the S&P futures was laid out. Welles studied the chart and then Jim put down the same chart with his projections and turning points and asked Welles to study it for a minute.

To Welles's amazement, he was able to comprehend what he saw in the overlay with colored lines and numbers. The turning points in the markets, what Jim wanted to show Welles, were becoming obvious. Over the next several hours, Jim showed Welles 15 bar charts and 15 different commodities under the projection of the colored lines and numbers.

Now, each turning point was not precise to the exact day, but they were close, almost within two to three days in most cases. Jim was quite sure of his discovery and that it would continue as in the past and into the future because what causes it never changes. Markets repeat directly or inversely relative to the total interaction of the sun, the moon, and the Earth.

According to the Delta Phenomenon, there are five time frames in which the markets repeat directly or inversely:

- Short-Term Delta (STD): Every four revolutions of the Earth; that is, every four days.
- Intermediate-Term Delta (ITD): Every four revolutions of the moon around the Earth; that, is every four lunar months.
- Medium-Term Delta (MTD): Every complete tidal cycle; that is, every lunar year.
- Long-Term Delta (LTD): Every four revolutions of the Earth around the sun: every four calendar years.
- Super Long-Term Delta (SLTD): Every complete total interaction of the sun, moon, and Earth: every 19 years and 5 hours.

Between the time frames, each market or commodity has a number count for turning points that relates specifically to that particular market. For simplicity's sake, I am not going to go into details about the counts between the Deltas but simply explain that each market has its own characteristic count in relation to the interaction of the sun, the moon, and the Earth.

Personally, I watch the Intermediate-Term Delta (ITD), which is every four revolutions of the moon around the Earth, which is every four lunar months. Figure 11.1 shows a chart of the S&P futures with the lines that represent the full moon cycle.

As you observe the chart in Figure 11.1, can you see a pattern with relation to the full moon and the points in between? Notice that the market's turning points come very close, most of the time,

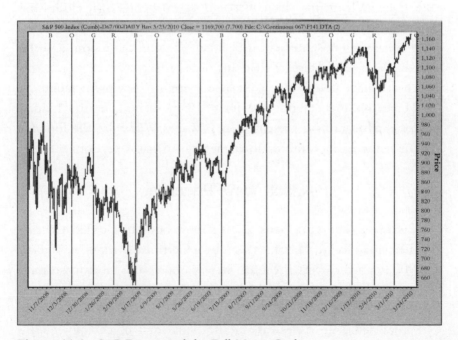

Figure 11.1   S&P Futures and the Full Moon Cycle
Source: Permission to use One Day at a Time Software given by J. Welles Wilder Jr., Delta Society International, www.DeltaSociety.com.

to the full moon. Now remember, Welles was shown this concept in 1983 and I have displayed a most recent chart of the S&P futures. The order of the universe seems to consistently, within reason, show turning points not only on or near the full moon but also between the full moons.

Years ago, I had a client who was an emergency room nurse. I remember back when we met in the late 1980s that she told me the busiest night in the emergency room was on a full moon. That stuck in my head, and when I learned of the Delta Phenomenon in 1999, it reminded me of my conversation with her. Even a movie produced and released in 1941 depicted the effect of the full moon on people: "The Wolf Man," starring Lon Chaney Jr. as the Wolf Man.

The full moon, bright in the sky, has always fascinated me. It has its own natural order and cycle that affects the earth and creates the tides. Why it has the effect it does on people still eludes me to this day. But, the fact remains that there is an order to the universe related to the interaction between the sun, the moon, and the Earth. We need to respect that this order affects markets as markets are really made up of participants and therefore have predictability.

Find out more about the Delta Phenomenon, or the hidden order in all markets as presented by J. Welles Wilder Jr., the founder of the Delta Society International, at www.deltasociety.com.

Elliott Wave Principle

In 2002, I picked up a book at an airport bookstore called *Conquer the Crash* that had just been written by a Certified Market Technician (CMT) named Robert Prechter. It was one of the most interesting concepts I had read about since learning about technical market analysis in my Bear Stearns days.

I learned a great deal about the behavioral psychology of the markets as Prechter presented the works of Ralph Nelson Elliott in a fascinating and convincing way. Elliott was a student of the stock market. He once wrote that "there is a reason for everything, and it is [one's] duty to try to discover it." Much of Elliott's work was in defining the concept of chaos in the markets.

In *Conquer the Crash*, Prechter describes a formative time in Elliott's career:

> In May 1934 . . . Elliott's observations of stock market behavior began coming together into a general set of principles that applied to all degrees of wave movement in the stock price averages. Today's scientific term for a large part of Elliott's observation about markets is that they are "fractal," coming under the umbrella of chaos science, although he went further in actually describing the component patterns and how they linked together. The former expert organizer of businesses had uncovered, through meticulous study, the organizational principle behind the movement of markets.

Prechter went on to collaborate with a financial advisor named Charles J. Collins on a book titled *The Wave Principle*, which was published in 1938.

The first chapter of *The Wave Principle* makes the following statements:

> No truth meets more general acceptance than that the universe is ruled by law. Without law, it is self-evident there would be chaos, and where chaos is, nothing is. . . . Very extensive research in connection with . . . human activities indicates that practically all developments which result from our social-economic processes follow a law that causes them to repeat themselves in similar and constantly recurring serials of waves or impulses of definite number and pattern. . . The stock market illustrates the wave impulse common to social-economic activity. . . It has its law, just as is true of other things throughout the universe.

In 1938, Elliott began publishing letters that analyzed and forecasted the path of the stock market. The Wave Principle was taking hold. By the early 1940s, Elliott had developed concepts incorporating human emotions and activities that followed a natural progression governed by laws of nature. He then coupled the patterns of his research of collective human behavior to the Fibonacci, or golden, ratio, a mathematical phenomenon known for millennia by mathematicians, scientists, artists, architects, and philosophers as nature's always-present laws of form and progress.

Elliott published his final work called *Nature's Law—The Secret of the Universe* in 1946. In it, he included almost every thought he had concerning the theory of the Wave Principle. Today, institutional portfolio managers, traders, and private investors continue to follow advancements to the Wave Principle through the publications of Robert Prechter's Elliott Wave International. I encourage you to learn more about the Elliott Wave Principles through Robert Prechter's writings and Elliott Wave International at www.elliottwave.com.

Prechter and Elliott Wave International

Robert Prechter, a certified market technician (CMT) and a former Technical Market Specialist with the Merrill Lynch market analysis department in New York, took a very strong understanding of Elliott's principle of market behavior. In 1979, he began publishing the monthly *Elliott Wave Theorist*, describing and explaining the wave theory over short, medium, and long-term periods. Currently he is president of Elliott Wave International, which publishes analyses of global stock, bond, currency, metals, and energy markets.

Prechter has won numerous awards for market timing, including the U.S. Trading Championship, and in 1989 was awarded the "Guru of the Decade" title by Financial News Network (now CNBC). He has been named "one of the premier timers in stock market history" by *Timer Digest*, "the champion market forecaster" by *Fortune* magazine, "the world leader in Elliott Wave interpretation" by The Securities Institute, and "the nation's foremost proponent of the Elliott Wave method of forecasting" by the *New York Times*.

Prechter is author, coauthor, or editor of 13 books, including *Elliott Wave Principle—Key to Market Behavior*, *R. N. Elliott's Masterworks*, *The Wave Principle of Human Social Behavior and the New Science of Socionomics*, *Conquer the Crash*, and *Pioneering Studies in Socionomics*.

Elliott Wave International (EWI) is the world's largest market forecasting firm. EWI's 20-plus analysts provide around-the-clock forecasts of every major market in the world via the Internet and proprietary web systems like Reuters and Bloomberg. EWI's educational services include conferences, workshops, webinars, videotapes, special reports, books, and one of the Internet's richest free-content programs, Club EWI.

Summary

Under the Wave Principle, progressions of the market's movements higher or lower occur naturally in mostly five-wave patterns. These movements generate forms in which these patterns have the ability to become predictable values. As the market can appear to reflect outside conditions and events, it can also, at other times, detach from the assumed conditions and move based on a law of its own. These movements or unfolding waves are patterns of directional movement that naturally occur under the wave principle.

In markets, movements take the form of five waves of a specific structure. Three of these waves, which are labeled 1, 3, and 5, actually affect the directional movement. They are separated by two countertrend waves labeled 2 and 4, as shown in Figure 11.2. The two interruptions are apparently essential for overall directional movement to occur.

At any time, the market may be identified as being somewhere in the basic five-wave pattern during a degree of a trend. Because

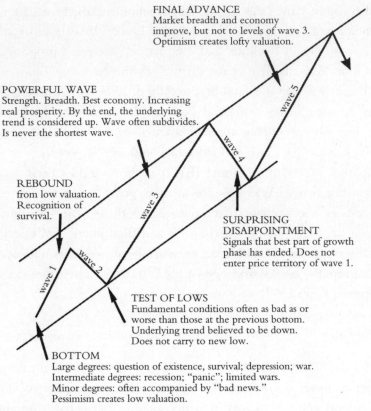

FINAL ADVANCE
Market breadth and economy
improve, but not to levels of wave 3.
Optimism creates lofty valuation.

POWERFUL WAVE
Strength. Breadth. Best economy. Increasing
real prosperity. By the end, the underlying
trend is considered up. Wave often subdivides.
Is never the shortest wave.

REBOUND
from low valuation.
Recognition of
survival.

wave 5

wave 4

wave 3

wave 1

wave 2

**SURPRISING
DISAPPOINTMENT**
Signals that best part of growth
phase has ended. Does not
enter price territory of wave 1.

TEST OF LOWS
Fundamental conditions often as bad as or
worse than those at the previous bottom.
Underlying trend believed to be down.
Does not carry to new low.

BOTTOM
Large degrees: question of existence, survival; depression; war.
Intermediate degrees: recession; "panic"; limited wars.
Minor degrees: often accompanied by "bad news."
Pessimism creates low valuation.

Figure 11.2   Elliott Wave Characteristics
SOURCE: Robert R. Prechter Jr., *Conquer The Crash*, John Wiley & Sons, Inc., 2002, Figure 3.9,
page 30. © 1980/2002 Elliott Wave International.

the five-wave pattern is the overriding form of market progress, all
other patterns are included within it.

Elliott believes the stock market unfolds according to a basic
rhythm or pattern of five waves up and three waves down to form a
complete cycle of eight waves. The five waves up are considered the
motive waves whereas the three waves down are considered corrective waves.

Elliott categorizes all waves by relative size or degree. He distin-
guished nine degrees of waves, from the smallest wiggle on an hourly
chart to the largest wave he could assume existed from the data then

available. He chose the names listed below to label these degrees, from largest to smallest:

- Grand Supercycle
- Supercycle
- Cycle
- Primary
- Intermediate
- Minor
- Minute
- Minuette
- Subminuette

It is important to understand that these labels refer to specifically identifiable degrees of waves.

In the February 2010 monthly issue of the *Elliott Wave Financial Forecast Report*, using Elliott Wave Principles with the Dow Jones Industrial Average, Robert Prechter forecasts that the markets are in a Grand Supercycle wave with the direction down, which began on January 14, 2000, and on which his optimum strategy is to preserve capital. He further describes the markets, in this Supercycle wave, as a depression under way. Finally, Prechter forecasts that we are in a Cycle that began on October 11, 2007 with direction down and also with an optimum strategy of holding cash.

Using my own analysis that includes the Elliott Wave Principles, I concur with Robert Prechter that the current layout of the cycles is indicating a deflationary depression is in progress. The cycle has the potential to bring the Dow Jones Industrial Average and the broader market indexes down into a low between 2012–2014, which has been my theme throughout this book. There are many ways to profit from such a cycle if you believe in the Elliott Wave Theory and Robert Prechter's analysis.

One way to profit would be to hedge your long positions with short positions. Another method would be to use invest-ment instruments such as exchange-traded funds (ETFs) or stock index futures that would profit from the market averages moving lower.

If you would like to learn more about the Elliott Wave Principles, I strongly encourage you to visit Elliott Wave International (www .elliottwave.com).

Fibonacci Numbers

The Fibonacci numbers are a sequence, not a series, of numbers uncovered by Leonardo "Fibonacci" da Pisa, a thirteenth-century mathematician. In the early 1200s, Fibonacci published *Liber Abaci,* a book of calculations that introduced his mathematical discoveries including the decimal system. This system included the positioning of zero as the first number in the number scale that became known as the Hindu-Arabic system, used today around the world.

The Fibonacci sequence starts with the digits 0 and 1, and then progresses to the next number by adding the last two numbers in the series together. Therefore, the sum of 0 and 1 is 1. Continuing with this mathematical concept, we then get $1 + 1 = 2$; $2 + 1 = 3$; $3 + 2 = 5$; $5 + 3 = 8$; $8 + 5 = 13$ and so on. The mathematical series then creates a sequence of numbers: 0; 1; 2; 3; 5; 8; 13; 21; 34; 55; 89; 144; 233; 377; 610; 987; 1,597; and so on.

Special Relationship of the Fibonacci Sequence

There is a further magical relationship in the Fibonacci sequence that Elliott from the Elliott Wave Theory called the Golden Ratio. After the first several numbers in the sequence (after 5), the ratio of any number to the next-higher number is approximately 1.618 times the number preceding it. The higher the number, the closer it approximates this ratio. Furthermore, any given number in the sequence approximates .618 of the following number. Between alternate numbers in the sequence, the second-higher number approximates

2.618 times the first number (i.e., 233 versus 89). Also, between the alternate numbers, the second number down creates a ratio of .382, the inverse of 2.618, to the first number (i.e., 55 versus 144). These relationships remain constant throughout the sequence.

1.618 (or .618) is also known as the golden mean. Its proportions seem to be pleasing to the eye and play an important role in the phenomena of music, art, architecture, and biology. William Hoffer, writing for the December 1975 *Smithsonian Magazine*, said:

> . . . the proportion of .618034 to 1 is the mathematical basis for the shape of playing cards and the Parthenon, sunflowers and snail shells, Greek vases and the spiral galaxies of outer space. The Greeks based much of their art and architecture upon this proportion. They called it "the golden mean."

The continual occurrence of Fibonacci numbers and the golden spiral in nature could explain, in mathematical form, why the proportion of .618034 to 1 is so pleasing in art. Any length can be divided in such a way that the ratio between the smaller part and the larger part is equivalent to the ratio between the larger part and the whole. That ratio is always .618.

Science is rapidly demonstrating that there is indeed a basic proportional principle of nature. By the way, your hand has *five* appendages, all but one of which have *three* jointed parts, *five* digits at the end, and *three* jointed sections to each digit.

Fibonacci Sequences and the Stock Market

The stock market's patterns are repetitive and fractal by nature. The same basic pattern of movement continues to show up in minor waves, using hourly plots all the way to Elliott's description of Supercycles and Grand Supercycles using yearly plots. Figure 11.3 reflects the hourly fluctuations in the Dow over a 10-day period from June 25–July 10, 1962 and shows a yearly plot of the S&P 500 Index from 1932–1978. Both plots indicate similar patterns of

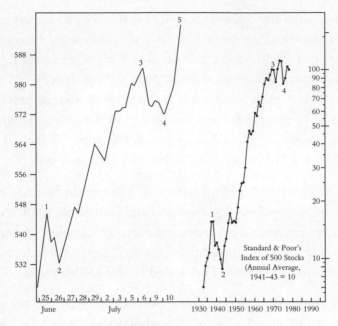

Figure 11.3 DJIA Hourly 1962 (S&P Yearly)
SOURCE: Courtesy of the *Media General Financial Weekly* from Elliott Wave International.
Reprinted with permission.

movement despite a difference in the time span of over 1500 to 1. In this example, the long-term formulation is still unfolding, but to date the pattern is along lines parallel to the hourly chart. This is because in the stock market, form is not a matter of the time element. Using the Elliott Wave Principles, both short- and long-term plots reflect a 5-3 relationship that can be aligned with the form that reflects the properties of the Fibonacci sequence of numbers. This suggests that collectively, man's emotions for investing can be expressed in the mathematical law of nature.

Continuing along nature's laws of mathematics, let's compare the formations shown in Figures 11.4 and 11.5. Each illustrates the natural law of the inwardly directed golden spiral of the Fibonacci sequence and is governed by the Fibonacci ratio. Each wave relates to the previous wave by .618. In fact, the distances in terms of the Dow points themselves reflect Fibonacci mathematics. In Figure 11.4

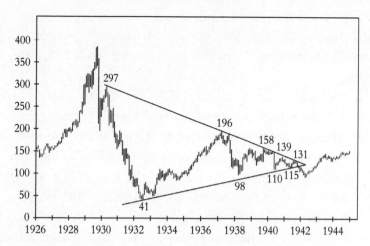

Figure 11.4 Fibonacci Retracements in the Dow Industrials, 1930–1941
SOURCE: Courtesy of the *Media General Financial Weekly* from Elliott Wave International.
Reprinted with permission.

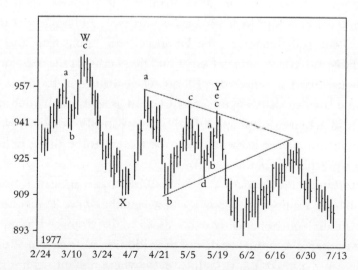

Figure 11.5 Fibonacci Lengths in a Symmetrical Triangle
SOURCE: Courtesy of the *Media General Financial Weekly* from Elliott Wave International.
Reprinted with permission.

showing the 1930–1941 sequence, the market swings cover approximately 260, 160, 100, 60, and 38 points respectively, closely resembling the declining list of Fibonacci ratios 2.618, 1.618, 1.00, .618 and .382.

Starting with wave X in the 1977 upward correction shown in Figure 11.5, the swings are almost exactly 55 points (wave X), 34 points (waves a through c), 21 points (wave d), 13 points (wave a of e) and 8 points (wave b of e), the Fibonacci sequence itself. The total net gain from beginning to end is 13 points, and the apex of the triangle lies exactly on the level of the correction's beginning at 930, which is also the level of the peak of the subsequent reflex rally in June. Whether you take the actual number of points in the waves as coincidence or part of the design, you can be certain that the precision manifest in the constant .618 ratio between each successive wave is not coincidence.

The spiral-like form of market action is repeatedly shown to be governed by the golden ratio, and even Fibonacci numbers appear in market statistics more often than mere chance. However, it is crucial to understand that while the numbers themselves do have theoretic weight in the grand concept of the Wave Principle, it is the *ratio* that is the fundamental key to growth patterns of this type. Although it is rarely pointed out in the literature, the Fibonacci ratio results from this type of additive sequence no matter what two numbers start the sequence.

In its broadest sense, the Elliott Wave Principle proposes that the same law that shapes living creatures and galaxies is inherent in the spirit and activities of people. The Elliott Wave Principle shows up clearly in the market because the stock market is the finest reflector of mass psychology in the world.

In Robert Prechter's and Elliott Wave International's opinion, with which I agree, the parallels between the Wave Principle and other natural phenomena are too great to be dismissed as just so much nonsense. On the balance of probabilities, we have come to the conclusion that there is a principle, everywhere present, giving shape to social affairs, and that Einstein knew what he was talking about when he said, "God does not play dice with the universe." The stock market is no exception, as mass behavior is undeniably linked to a law that can be studied and defined. The briefest way to express this principle is a simple mathematical statement: the 1.618 ratio.

Terry Laundry's T Theory

Terry Laundry lives and works out of Nantucket Island, Massachusetts, far from the noise of Wall Street. He is a former marine with extensive discipline training, and he has an engineering degree from MIT. His engineering mind and discipline enabled Terry to develop skills to analyze the markets and figure out that the markets spend the same amount of time going up as they do going down, hence the T in T Theory.

Terry lives and breathes T Theory. He publicly shares his thoughts daily and weekly on his web sites: www.ttheoryfoundation .org for tutorials and daily update and www.ttheory.com for his big-picture T Theory Sunday Observations. I share this very interesting and important cycle tool because it may help you visualize the future probability of price movements in the broader markets. As we know, nothing is for sure or perfect, but the historical analysis using T Theory holds up to its probable predictions. On his web sites, Terry shows historical Ts that provide insight into his theories from past analysis. My respect for Terry is from his constant updating, where he not only gives the T Theory perspective but also discusses the possibility of the wrong Ts.

For many years, I had observed that the markets had some type of symmetry but I just didn't have the ability to see it as clearly as Terry presents it. I quickly came to understand the concept of his T Theory as I had for years thought that the markets mirror or image history repeating itself from a short- and longer-term pattern perspective that can be recognized or decoded through symmetry.

In T Theory, Terry incorporates the technical indicators that I watch, as well as his own proprietary indicators, and observes peaks and valleys in them to draw the T formation. Once the T formation is recognized from the left side of the T, the right side of the T, as determined by Terry, may have predictions of tremendous value in determining what may be in the future. The time frames for the T can be as short as weeks to as long as decades. But, most importantly, the T Theory method measures the time frame of where the end of the symmetry of a market may occur in the future, which to me is most important. My opinion has been that it is easy to get into a trade or invest in the markets but it's the exit strategy that is most important. T Theory incorporated into your own methodology can give additional guidance as your ability to see cycles and patterns develops, but where we are now in the cycles is of most importance.

An opinion that Terry and I share is that the equity markets are due for a major low in the near future, as I have been writing throughout this book and in my own *Shaffer Market Report*, which I issue twice a week. My target for the next cycle low is between 2012 and 2014, and I believe it will be caused by a deflationary depression cycle that may have only just begun. This may also coincide with the approximate 40-year cycle that Terry and I both agree on. Figure 11.6 is a chart

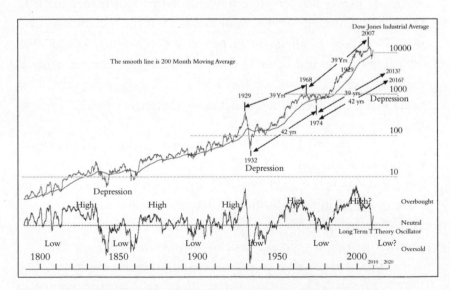

Figure 11.6   The Long-Range T Theory 40-Year Cycle
SOURCE: Copyright 2010 by T Theory Foundation, Inc. at www.ttheoryfoundation.org.

created by Terry that shows his view and prediction of the depression cycle that he currently illustrates as a cycle bottoming between 2013 and 2016. My current target for the eventual low in the Dow Jones Industrial Average is approximately 3,500. As you observe on Terry's chart, he also is predicting the target low somewhere in the same area.

Terry and I also have similar thoughts about the price of gold long term. We both agree that gold is in a bull market with his T Theory predicting a high around the year 2020. I, though, predict that as the equity markets fall into a cycle low that the price of gold along with other asset classes will retreat to lower levels due to a deflationary depression cycle before stabilizing and moving higher. Currently, my expectation for the price of gold is around the $800 an ounce area before it resumes its long-term trend into our predicted 2020 high of its cycle. The year 2020 may be part of an inflation cycle but for right now we need to get to a bottom before inflation is anywhere near an issue. Figure 11.7 shows Terry's predictive long-term T Theory chart of the price of gold.

Finally, Terry is currently predicting a short-term cycle high using T Theory into August of 2010 as shown in Figure 11.8. I'm

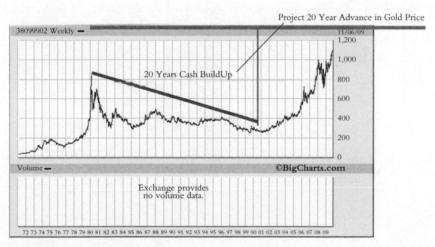

Figure 11.7   Big Gold T

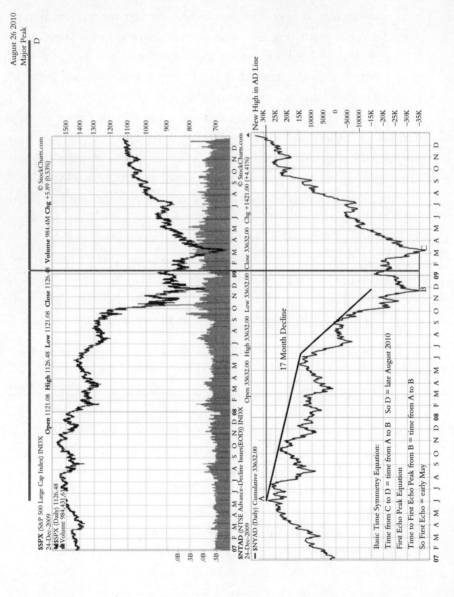

Figure 11.8 Advance–Decline T #13

not so sure we may get this cycle high, as I believe the highs may have already been reached with a 50 percent plus retracement in the Dow Jones Industrial Average and the S&P 500. Below is Terry's current short-term view of the market for 2010. Either way, we both agree a lower market is ahead for many years to come.

In conclusion, I encourage you to review Terry Laundry's web sites and review the available tutorials on the concepts of T Theory including his daily and Sunday observations. He is also available by e-mail and he does respond through his weekly Sunday Observation audio clips. The T Theory concept may give you a view of the markets that you have never seen before.

Summary

I have presented three great cycle concepts in this chapter that all seem to point in one way or another to a declining stock market and a low inflation environment for, in my opinion, years to come. They all seem to correlate to a 40-year cycle in which the stock market in the United States ultimately found deep lows.

My target for the next expected low is between 2012 and 2014 as I have been discussing throughout this book. I suspect 2013 will be the toughest year financially for not just the stock market but for businesses and households alike. The question is, what do you do if my predicted deflationary cycle or depression does materialize?

Of course you should consult your own financial advisor but here are a few suggestions, which of course will depend on your personal level of risk and experience. First, I would currently be liquidating hard assets such as precious metals, real estate, and other assets that would have a hard time finding buyers if all asset classes are to be sold to raise cash. This does not mean sell your house, unless you believe that you can buy it back cheaper later and you have somewhere else to live, but I am referring to investment holdings that do not have a readily liquid market. If the economy slows down and the velocity of money declines in such a dramatic fashion, then people will be selling any asset they can just to raise cash. Try to get ahead of the curve.

Secondly, if invested in stocks that you have the ability to watch, I would pay close attention to the price action and create an exit strategy for when you feel you have had enough of giving back profits or are not willing to take any further losses. An exit strategy might do you some good as you may never have had one before. As far as equity mutual funds are concerned, I would recommend liquidating those funds and buying individual stocks that you could personally watch. Mutual funds, if the markets start to fall, are mostly mandated to be fully invested and you give total control to the management style of the particular mutual fund you are invested in. An alternative would be to have an individually managed account with a manager whose philosophy and style you agree with. An individual account gives you the ability to see your holding and performance on a daily or live basis as it is your account that the manager is overseeing. You also should have the ability to talk directly to the manager if you have any concerns and have the ability to liquidate your account or cut down your exposure immediately upon request.

Third, if you are invested in bond funds, I would recommend getting out of these funds as they are perpetual in nature, which means that they never mature. A bond fund is similar to a stock or equity fund in which you solely rely on the manager to make decisions as to the holdings. Owning individual bonds gives you not only the opportunity to know what you actually own but also a maturity date. Not similar to bond funds, which have the tendency to go down if the interest rate environment experiences a rise in rates, individual bonds, regardless of the fluctuations of interest rates, give you a definite maturity date as long as the issuer is solvent and can pay. This gets to my next point. As of the writing of this book, I have a major concern about the safety and risk levels of municipal bonds and corporate bonds. Municipalities, during an economic slowdown, may have financial problems that could lead to a disruption of interest payments or principal payments when the bonds become due.

I also have concern about corporate bonds as these bonds could also be affected by a deflationary depression. No matter what the rating agencies say, and we all know the accuracy of those organizations, use your own judgment or that of a professional advisor to determine the various risk levels of the issuers.

Finally, for those of you who are more risky, there are exchange-traded funds (ETFs) that take advantage of a falling stock market on not only the major indexes but also on selected sectors that may fall faster than the broader market. Again, I would suggest that you consult a professional advisor as to the workings of these instruments but they certainly can give your portfolio either some protection as a hedge to your current long holdings if you choose to hold them or give you some octane to take advantage of my prediction of a much lower stock market over the coming years.

Looking farther out, once we have come through a declining economic period and stock market, there are opportunities to take advantage of the next cycle which at this point is years away. An example would be that during the low point of this predicted cycle, gold and those hard assets that you are selling now could again become major assets in your portfolio for the final outcome to this cycle, which would most likely be, in my opinion, runaway inflation or hyperinflation as the government may not be able to control the overspending of dollars that is their current policy.

Chapter 12

Engineering of the Markets

C hapter 12 is important to help you navigate your portfolio through economic storms. These techniques are useful during manias, bubbles, hyperinflation, and other economic scenarios. Instead of the buy-and-hold style of investing, which didn't work from 2000 to 2009 as some indexes lost value during that period, I suggest moving in and out of the markets to capture profits. This is the type of activity that day traders and short-term traders manage to do every day. Traders that make a living on market movements have disciplined trading models or methods that give them the edge to profit especially during economic storms. On a daily basis, the day traders who make a living trading the markets engineer movements which create profit opportunities. We may be in a period of a trading market similar to the 1970s and 1950s where the market indexes moved sideways to lower for many years.

Did you ever wonder why, as you were watching or studying price movements, a particular investment topped out at a given area or bottomed out at a given area? Well, you are not alone. Through years of experience watching market movements, I have come to realize that engineering of the markets exists. Similar to the laws that we follow for driving a car, professional day traders follow a code or rules for profiting during the trading day. When a day trader comes to work in the morning, in order to have an edge for profitability, he needs a game plan, similar to a road map. And this road map must be adhered to by other traders in order for it to have the potential for making profits consistently. So in effect, a code has been put together and passed around among all who wish to follow it to make money.

Let me give you some details. A very common formula for trading during the day to find areas of interest to either buy or sell is known as the "floor trader's pivot points." Simply put, it is a mathematical calculation that has absolutely no meaning.

It's like the U.S. Tax Code for Alternative Minimum Tax. The reason the calculation works most of the time is because the users, which are many, follow these formulas and trade accordingly.

The Floor Trader's Pivot Points

In its simplest terms, the floor trader pivot points or trend reaction numbers are nothing more than numbers, based on the previous day's trading performance, that inform investors of what the market should be doing in terms of maintaining equilibrium.

The formula (remember, we are using yesterday's values to calculate today's expectations) is as follows: First, calculate the pivot point, which is X. This is the center of the new day's trading activity and it is incorporated into further calculations:

$$\text{High} + \text{Low} + \text{Close} / 3 = X$$

Then, using the pivot point of X, calculate the Expected Low and Expected High of the new day as:

$$2X - High = Expected Low$$
$$2X - Low = Expected High$$

Finally, calculate the Expected Lowest Low and the Expected Highest High of the new day as:

$$High - Low = Y$$
$$X - Y = Expected Lowest Low$$
$$X + Y = Expected Highest High$$

These are the five areas of interest to look out for during the new trading day:

1. Expected Highest High
2. Expected High
3. Pivot Point
4. Expected Low
5. Expected Lowest Low

Now, let's put these formulas to work in real time. Using the above calculations, we will use January 6, 2010 data to predict January 7, 2010 areas of expected interest using the S&P 500 Index:

High = 1136.75
Low = 1133.94
Close = 1137.14

Step 1 is:

$$1139.18(High) + 1133.94(Low) + 1137.14(Close) / 3$$
$$= 1136.75 \text{ or our } X$$

Step 2 is:

$$2 \times 1136.75(X) - 1139.18(\text{High}) = 1134.33 \text{ (Expected Low)}$$
$$2 \times 1136.75(X) - 1133.94(\text{Low}) = 1139.57 \text{ (Expected High)}$$

And, finally, Step 3 is:

$$1139.18(\text{High}) - 1133.94(\text{Low}) = 5.24 \text{ or our Y}$$
$$1136.75(X) - 5.24(Y) = 1131.51 \text{ (Expected Lowest Low)}$$
$$1136.75(X) + 5.24(Y) = 1141.99 \text{ (Expected Highest High)}$$

Thus, the calculations for the engineering expectations for January 7, 2010 are as follows:

- Expected Highest High = 1141.99
- Expected High = 1139.57
- Pivot Point = 1136.75
- Expected Low = 1134.33
- Expected Lowest Low = 1131.51

Figure 12.1 illustrates the five-minute movements in the S&P 500 for January 7, 2010. The horizontal lines represent the five areas of interest that we calculated from the previous day's values of January 6, 2010 using the preceding formulas.

As shown on the five-minute S&P 500 Index chart for January 7, 2010, the market opened below the pivot point of 1136.75 and within 20 minutes of trading the index quickly moved to the Expected Low of 1134.33, which did not hold. The index then tested the Expected Lowest Low of 1131.51, for which it found support within 30 minutes of trading. About 35 minutes later, a test of the Expected Low of 1134.33 was reached to the upside and buying came in to bring the index up even further above the Pivot Point of 1136.75. The trading range between the Expected High of 1139.57 and Pivot Point of 1136.75 was experienced from around 11:00 P.M. until 2:30 P.M. as this is usually the time the traders take

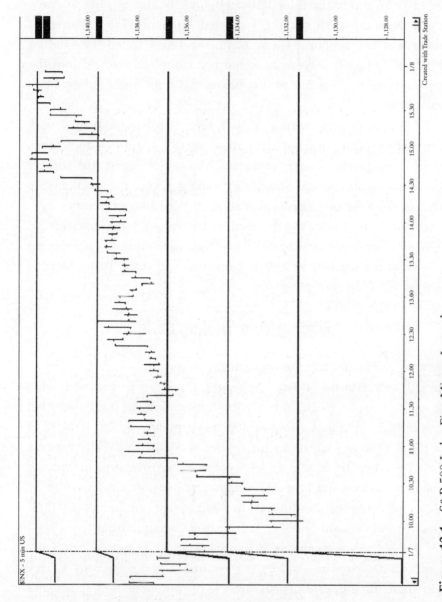

Figure 12.1 S&P 500 Index Five-Minute Intervals

lunch across the country considering several time zone differences. After 2:30 P.M., the index then broke through the Expected High of 1139.57 and tested the Highest High of the day of 1141.99, then came back down to test the Expected High of 1139.57 to see if there was any support. Then, again, the index tested the Highest High of 1141.99, and finally found resistance and sold off into the close of the trading day to just below the Expected Highest High calculation.

Now that's engineering! I have seen this basic formula work most of the time on many daily movements for indexes, indicators, stocks, commodities, and currencies. I strongly suggest that you try this formula on your investments or trading as you, too, will observe that most of the time these calculations are great target points.

This formula can also be applied for longer term investors on a weekly, monthly, and yearly basis. But, bottom line, engineering occurs in the markets on a daily basis and even yearly basis, depending on who's in control.

Finding Your Trading Style

Several years ago I had the opportunity to meet the legendary champion trader, Martin "Buzzy" Schwartz. For those of you who don't know of him, in 1983, he made the most money in trades reported to the U.S. Trading Championship: $1.4 million, which resulted in a 175.3 percent increase in his futures account. In a 1984 contest, he won when he returned 254.9 percent and thereafter he entered the next contest and beat 262 entrants by increasing his account by 443.7 percent return in futures. In 1992 he won the new $500,000-plus futures division of the U.S. Investing Championship.

Buzzy was a securities analyst, and at 33 years old, with the support of his wife Audrey—a beautiful person whom I have also had the opportunity to meet—he put pencil to paper and decided to become a trader, as he explains in his book *Pit Bull: Lessons from Wall Street's Champion Trader*, published in 1998. He writes that nothing fit his personality better and there was nothing he enjoyed more. He continues to explain in his book that he was good with math, quick with figures, loved gambling, and loved the market. He was right to study the methods and styles of trading that worked for him.

To this day, from his home in Florida, he continues to trade and follows the methods that fit his personality. He realized early on from his previous trading that going for the knockout trade had made him a loser for nine years before he met his wife Audrey. He developed his methodology and style of getting in and out of his trades quickly. He also learned to get out of losing trades quickly to clear his head for the next trade.

In my first encounter with Buzzy in 2007, he was a gentleman. As we sat down for lunch he immediately handed me sheets of paper that he had prepared titled "Notes for Book" and "Things to Remind About." He explained to me that these thoughts and ideas would be helpful in understanding some of the characteristics of the market. Early on in his trading career he had a mentor that helped him and I certainly feel that in his way he was mentoring me.

This section includes advice from the champion trader on finding your trading style and how to profit in bad and good markets.

Observations from a Top Day Trader

Here are some great trading and market observations that Buzzy Schwartz shared with me and I now share with you:

- Buy the rumors and sell the news.
- Money usually comes into the markets (and into commodity futures) at the beginning, middle, and end of the month.
- When markets open weak, they usually close weak.
- When markets open strong, they usually close strong.
- The 5-minute stochastic (a day trader's indicator) is the key for entry and exit of a trade indicating when to buy and sell. It is especially an effective tool on trend days.

- On a strong trending day when the 5-minute stochastic is able to recoup 50 percent, that may be the signal to enter the trend (it is probably your only chance).
- Stocks usually make a low on the Thursday or Friday (second of the month) before option expiration (third Friday of the month).
- At the S&P 500 expiration, the open is driven up for cash settlement and then goes down during the day and may rally again for the close when the components expire.
- The markets bottom on the Monday or Tuesday before the end of the quarter so that they (money managers, mutual funds, and the like) can mark the market up for the end of the quarter on Wednesday, Thursday, or Friday.
- At the beginning of the month/quarter, buy or sell programs usually do not coincide with the market opening, but occur at 10:00 A.M. New York time.
- A top often occurs in the first week of the new quarter.
- The market tends to rally with the New York lunchtime and lasts for about 30–60 minutes. It occurs somewhere between 11:30 A.M.–1:00 P.M. New York time.
- It is not usually a good idea to trade between 11:30 A.M. and noon. Trading at that time is known as a boredom trade and is often also a losing trade.
- Momentum direction changes can occur with each half hour of trading.
- The market can sell off for the first 15 minutes of a half-hour bracket and then run up for the last 15 minutes.
- The 10-week moving average acts as resistance when it is being crossed from below. The 10-week moving average acts as support when it is crossed from above. When the 10-week moving average flattens out it means that it may change direction and act as either support or resistance.
- When brokerage firms and banks are down significantly for the day, the market will follow suit.

- When the TRIN indicator is down a small amount and the Dow Jones is down, that could mean that the market will go down further. The TRIN indicator should be down twice as much as the Dow Jones.

  Note: TRIN = 5 short-term trading index which is a ratio: (Advancing Issues/Declining Issues) / (Advancing Volume/ Declining Volume)
- On a range-trading day it is best to do a fade trade, where you buy the low and sell the high.
- Inside days (where the high and low of the day are within the previous day's high and low range) are usually followed by great volatility, resulting in an outside day (where the high and low of the day exceed the previous day's high and low).
- Reversal days occur when a new low is made early in the day and is followed by a higher close. If the higher close does not occur then there is no significance. Inversely, reversals can also be a new high made early in the day followed by a close on the lows.
- When leading stocks are up a lot on the day, slowly continue to go up, and suddenly reverse bid to the downside, it means the bubble is bursting and the market may be ready to move down.
- A rising wedge pattern is formed by connecting the tops of the daily bar chart with a line and doing the same with the bottoms; when the index is close to the apex of the rising wedge it usually breaks to the downside, and often very sharply.
- Excess Money Growth = Money Growth − Growth of GDP
- If excess growth is large we know that the markets may rise as the excess has to go into the investment markets.
- If the market's secondary rally fizzles and then the market dumps again for the third time, the key is to watch if the market makes a new low or not.
- When the market is down and it rallies over lunchtime it is a countertrend.

- Asset Allocation = Sell stocks and buy bonds because they are changing the amount of equities they want to be exposed to. Bonds are fixed-income vehicles that reduce exposure to stocks.
- Sometimes with the official close of the U.S. Treasury bond market futures at 3:00 P.M. New York time, the stock market stops going down (stop selling) because asset allocation managers can no longer buy bonds (as the after market gets quiet and thin).
- The Globex or overnight trading range of futures acts as support and resistance levels during normal trading hours.
- When the S&P futures open down and rally and then don't make it back to the previous day's close it is usually a signal to go short and that the market may go down.
- In a bear market, the market may try to rally early in the day and early in the week and then they sell off into the end of the week.
- If the market opens higher, sell a large gap up because the momentum/volume is used up at or near the opening of the market, and the market may sell off.

Take some of the points from the preceding list and incorporate them into your style of investing or trading. Essentially, the market times in cycles that can be identified regardless of the economic environment. Identify entry and exit points for your own investments using the engineering of the markets.

A year later, I had the opportunity to play a round of golf with Buzzy. It was such a pleasure to spend the hours together as he shared some of his thoughts about trading, the investment world, and perceptions in life. I strongly suggest that you get a copy of his book and read it cover to cover, as it has extremely valuable concepts and information that would encourage any trader or investor to gain self-confidence.

Identifying the Engineers

There are several ways to define the engineers of the markets. Every business morning when you awake, you can usually find a media outlet giving you the opening indications for the major stock market indexes through the use of the futures contracts. Futures on the major indexes trade electronically beginning on Sunday nights until Friday afternoons when they close for the weekend at 4:15 P.M. New York time. These futures contracts trade even though the underlying indexes are not trading, as the indexes only update during normal trading day session hours, currently 9:30 A.M. through 4:00 P.M. Eastern Time.

As defined by the Commodity Futures Trading Commission in the Commitment of Traders Report released every Friday, unless it falls on a holiday, there are three players in the futures markets (www.cftc.gov). First, there are the large speculators. These are defined as funds and individual traders that hold positions above the reporting threshold for speculative purposes only. Then, there are the commercials or hedgers. They are traders, market makers, or professional firms that are actually in the business of buying and selling the underlying securities for a business, and they use the futures markets to hedge their inventory of stocks if they are long by selling futures contracts to offset their exposure. Or, the commercials or hedgers can buy the futures contracts if they have a large amount of cash to put into the market to get a lower price now and slowly buy the stocks and sell off their long futures positions until they have achieved their goals. Finally, we are left with the small speculator who is the local mom and pop, dentist, small business owner, and so on, who has a small capitalized account with which they speculate on movements in the markets.

Now ever since I've been a trader, which dates back to 1983, I have found that the futures, most of the time, lead the cash index markets. They can lead in a split second. For example, if someone wanted to move the market higher, they could easily buy thousands of futures contracts, putting very little money down, and move the markets higher as the underlying stocks move higher to get the index closer to the trading price of the futures contract.

Can the markets be manipulated? I believe that to a certain extent there are those that have the ability and have been doing it for a long time. Nowadays, it doesn't take a lot of capital to move the index futures markets, as the leverage is quite attractive to the trading community.

There are also algorithmic trading programs or "black boxes" that have the ability to move prices around in a flash automatically, as we have experienced since the market topped in 2007. The manipulative trading programs can buy and sell, electronically, securities against futures contracts on a fully mechanical basis. This quick in-and-out use of these trading programs has come into the public light and has tampered with the reputation of Wall Street on Main Street USA. Some of the firms on Wall Street have been extremely profitable while other firms have not. I ask myself why the difference? Obviously something different is going on from one firm to another.

In more general terms, there are engineers in the market, whether on a daily, weekly, monthly, or even yearly basis, whose sole purpose is to profit from volatility and large price movements. According to the theme of this book, even these profiteers have something to do with the markets moving higher or lower, creating cycles, depending on how much money they would like to make and in which direction. Most of the time the path of least resistance is down, as was seen in our most recent decline from 2007 and during the well-known crash of 1929, where several wealthy individuals sold short the market and kept shorting the market until they were asked to stop by the authorities.

As history repeats itself, today the same activities take place in the markets that have taken place since their inception. The only difference is the technology, as greed continues to be a cornerstone of society. The emotional and psychological makeup of humans has not changed. Our goal is to try to share methods of isolating where and which cycle is taking place in your life. But always be conscious that there may be a stronger power than you moving prices around.

Chapter 13

The Bottom Line

I have reviewed quite a few topics in this book and I hope that you have found concepts and methods that you can apply to your own investment strategies. I also hope that I have added value to your psychological approach to investing in the markets. We all experience the greed, fear, and emotion of investing in different ways. Some view investing success as pure luck, while others give credit to probability. In this business, every trader will have winning trades as well as losing trades. As a longer term investor, you, too, will experience the winning and the losing trades. The results lie within as to handling them appropriately.

Recognizing Cycles Everywhere

Even though I present cycles in investment opportunities in the markets, I also hope that the analysis of the history of how the banking system, civilizations, and human nature play significant roles in these cycles can improve your life.

After all, our lives are also encompassed in cycles. We'd all like to know the precise timing for the end cycle, but of course we don't. As we move through life, consider the lengths and depths of cycles within your sphere and how they affect you day to day. You may find similarities between your bull and bear periods and the markets.

For example, seasonal cycles can affect our psychological thinking. In the winter when there is lots of snow and cold, many experience seasonal depression. Some may recognize it, some may even be treated for it, but it is a seasonal cycle that can be counted on.

What I believe is most important to you is that you are going through many different cycles within your own life and it's the recognition of these cycles and where you are in relation to them that may help you achieve what you would like out of life. Some of us may experience emotional cycles while others may experience business cycles, both of which affect your well-being as a human on this earth. Take note of what type of cycles you may be experiencing at this time and try to relate them to experiences that may have happened to you in previous years.

History does repeat itself and it is my belief that cycles are what cause the repeating of history. We cannot stop these natural cycles from occurring, but same as the markets, if we can identify them and define where we are in the cycle we can possibly explain some things that happen to us in our daily lives. This may lead to happier investment results and a happier life.

Whether you now realize it or not, you are in the midst of many natural cycles today. You are definitely experiencing a seasonal cycle as the seasons change. You are also experiencing the cycle of the moon without even realizing its effect. You are also in the cycle of the Earth, sun, and moon relationship.

You are going to experience the sunspot cycle increases, as they are on the upswing and greater numbers of solar flares from the sun are expected over the next few years. Solar energy affects the Earth and in some way may affect you the same as it effects weather patterns or stock market movements.

Furthermore, you are actually in the midst of an economic cycle that you may have not experienced before. How will this cycle affect you? It could be financially, emotionally, or in a different form.

Cycles are also going on around you. If you are watching TV, the screen functions on cycles to bring you the picture. The sound waves you hear are based on cycles. Dogs are known to hear higher levels of sounds that humans can't hear, hence the dog whistle (have you ever heard it?).

Continuing along this theme, you are physically being hit by radio wave cycles as they are transmitted in the air. This includes cell phones, AM and FM radio, your local police dispatcher, and during the daytime sunlight rays, as light is also on the cycle spectrum.

The bottom line: Cycles are part of our daily lives and cycles exist within the markets, and that is what causes financial depressions, deflation, hyperinflation and market bubbles. Plan your investments accordingly.

What to Do Right Now

As the United States rolls into a deflationary depression and credit availability becomes less, we can expect a slow rate of growth for the economy and the markets will price in appropriately. This cycle fits into my predicted 40-year stock market cycle low between 2012 and 2014. In a deflationary cycle, prices of consumer goods are expected to decline in the general economy. This suggests that corporate profit growth will be mediocre at best. Of course some companies will out-perform others, but as a whole, the general environment for goods and services will remain weak. Personal savings will become the buzz word on the landscape accompanied by less risk appetite by investors.

Cash will be king. Investing in cash or cash equivalents would be a good idea for those of you who do not have the appetite for risk at all. Such instruments for parking cash would be U.S. Treasury bills or notes. Try to stay on the short-term side as down the road inflation will begin to rise and longer term notes and bonds will reflect this change before it occurs. You may experience a loss of principal if you need to cash out early.

If you want to have the potential to profit during the deflationary economic storm, I would suggest taking a look at exchange-traded funds (ETFs) that have the ability to profit as the stock market declines. There are quite a few of these ETFs offered and they come in many different flavors. For instance, the basic ETFs for the indexes will move inversely proportionate to their underlying index. But, there are ETFs that have leverage, too, such as two times the indexes or even three times the indexes. Remember that the two and three times leverage against the index could lose you more money if it moves against you so I do suggest you consult a professional before putting your hard-earned dollars into these. There are also ETFs that are geared toward certain segments or industries in the economy that may be appealing to you. Either way, diversification within the available ETFs would be a wise decision. I would also suggest that you stay with the ETFs that have the greatest amount of volume traded daily, as this will give you liquidity in case you would like to exit or if you choose to swing trade in and out of the trend.

Also, there are stock index futures such as on the Dow Jones Industrial Average, the S&P 500 Index, the NASDAQ 100 Index and the Russell 2000 Index. You can put on a short position, but unlike the ETFs, you could lose more than your original investment, so again I emphasize that you consult with a professional before using futures. These are more risky but can give you greater opportunities to trade in and out of the market as liquidity is high.

Options on stocks, indexes, and futures are also available as a hedge or outright positioning for a decline. The only real major issue with options is that you pay a premium for time. The time can decay the value of the option if the market moves slowly. As a trading vehicle, options may be the right fit for you if you intend to trade in and out according to volatility. I recommend that if you are not familiar with the risks of options that you find a professional to assist you.

I also see an opportunity in **new** public non-traded real estate investment trusts (REITs). New REITs are just starting up and have no legacy assets from the previous real estate collapse, which means that they don't hold properties from years ago at higher prices. Also, because these public non-traded REITs are not listed on any exchange, they can have steady valuations verses publicly traded REITs whose stock prices move around based on stock market conditions. If my prediction of a lower stock market materializes, then publicly traded REIT stock prices may be put under pressure and decline even though the property values stay reasonable. I believe that new public non-traded REITs will become the next shadow banking system as they will be flush with cash to invest in properties that are put on the market at severely depressed prices. Our banking system will still be in stress over the next few years which will give public non-traded REITs tremendous buying opportunities.

I particularly like the public non-traded REITs that invest in retail and commercial properties. These particular REITs generate income from rent and they will be able to take advantage of my projected decline in commercial real estate prices. These new REITs being set up today are raising capital to buy distressed income properties from the sellers who may be forced to sell as their mortgages will be coming due in the next three years. These mortgages will be difficult to refinance due to the decrease in the property values. Accordingly, there are billions of dollars in commercial real estate loans coming due that banks and other lenders may not want to hold or refinance. REITs will be ready and willing to step up to purchase distressed income-producing properties as sellers scramble. REITs also must pay most of their income out to investors, so you will benefit from the income stream while at the same time have potential for gains on the real estate properties five to 10 years from now. I expect the inflation or hyperinflation cycle to develop after 2015, which fits the holding period of the properties in new

REITs. There are some new REITs today that expect to start selling their properties five to seven years from now. This could be a great opportunity for a potential gain in your investment along with income. Again, I suggest you consult an advisor qualified in discussing REITs with you.

What I would not do is stay fully invested in long only mutual funds that invest in equities. The buy-and-hold era has come to an end. The alternative, if you would like to stay involved in the markets and don't want to manage your portfolio yourself, would be to find a money manager that can invest for you through a separately managed account. This type of manager has the ability to get in and out of the markets as he actively manages your account. The manager should not have access to your funds in the account or hold your assets, only the ability to buy or sell investments for you. This separation can keep you out of trouble down the road if your manager decides to be another Ponzi scheme expert.

Up Next: Inflation or Hyperinflation

As the current cycle winds down to a deflationary depression, there is no place to go but to the next phase of the cycle. Eventually the U.S. economy will begin to heat up. Prices will start to rise as demand will outstrip supply. The cutbacks that we will experience for the next several years will cause shortages of goods. Shortage of goods means that the sellers can raise prices. Raising prices is an inflationary concern. I don't believe that it will be stoppable.

Therefore, during the next few years, as the low expectation of the economic cycle arrives, you may want to start accumulating hard assets such as raw materials. You can do this through ETFs or purchase of companies that are in the resource sector of the economy. But wait until the time is right. Today, it is too early to be chasing these ideas. I would be looking to buy into these sectors after 2013 if I were investing to hold for the several years after that.

My current expectation for gold is that it will be much higher than where it is now after the deflationary depression, but I would not buy it today. Wait until no one wants to buy gold or raw materials. That would be an optimal entry point. Of course you will never buy these sectors at the exact bottom. I recommend that you buy them on the way up once the bottom is clearer. Buy strength; don't try to pick a bottom.

The use of ETFs, futures, options, REITs, and professional managers will greatly enhance your opportunity to profit from the coming inflationary environment. There will be some false starts as our economy sputters back and forth until it catches fire again. The stock market will most likely remain a trader's or short term investor's market until the government gets out of the way and lets capitalism back in the door.

One of my reasons for the high inflationary cycle down the road is because of the uncertainty of the Federal Reserve Bank and its role going forward. I do not believe the current form of the bank will be around after 2013, which is its 100-year anniversary. The whole banking system in the United States may be reformed once the dust settles from the reality of what really occurred from 2000 to 2009. Damage to the financial system will take years to repair and years to gain trust from the people again. This will also keep most investors out of the stock market.

On a further note, I believe that the Euro Currency may not be around much after 2013, as it did not provide the sovereign wealth countries any protection from the economic storm. Countries may decide to go back to their original currencies over which they would have more control, thereby reducing the unity of the European Union. I don't believe that 16 separate countries with individual economies can function on a common currency. Each country needs its own currency to balance inflows and outflows of trade.

Finally, with the U.S. budget deficit climbing to sky-high levels, officials may find the answer to paying off the debt with a weakened dollar. Allowing interest rates to stay at low levels for an extended period of time will most likely give inflation teeth down the road. That means that the United States will be paying down debt with cheaper dollars as the dollar weakens. Watch out for this setup after 2014.

Take advantage of inflation by purchasing hard assets. From a U.S. investor's point of view, hard asset prices will climb especially because most assets are priced in U.S. dollars. Again, look at companies that would benefit from a weaker U.S. dollar after 2014. Also, I suggest looking at ETFs that specialize in holdings of hard assets. The leverage is up to you. Finally, I suggest a professional to guide you through the inflationary period, as it may become the most inflationary period in 50 years.

And Then: The New Bubble

After the intense period of inflation or hyperinflation, prices will become so high that it will have the characteristics of a bubble. You won't find the bubble in the stock market. It will appear in the hard assets market. What usually happens is that the assets are so inflated that producers pump out production at their highest levels to take advantage of the pricing.

More and more investors will pile into the rising assets as if there is no tomorrow. Prices will be expected to continue to climb, until the bubble bursts. History does repeat itself, as oversupply will take over and less demand will be evident. The result will be a burst of hard asset prices. As mentioned in an earlier chapter of the book, I expect gold to predict this period. Once gold makes a bottom in this current deflationary cycle, then it may rise to extreme heights ending around the year 2020. There will be a great opportunity to profit from the inflationary storm not only through gold but many of the other hard assets such as silver, crude oil, soybeans, corn, sugar and all the other staples we need in our daily lives.

Always remember that eventually the bubble will burst. Be prepared. Don't get caught up in the frenzy, instead sell into the frenzy. As many investment managers say, buy when nobody wants it and sell when everybody needs it. Good words to invest by.

Summary

I am predicting a deflationary depression for the next few years with asset prices, stock market prices, real estate prices, and interest rates on U.S. Treasuries yields to remain low or move lower into the 2012–2014 period. Then, a gradual increase in pricing as inflation starts to enter the economic cycle after 2014. The U.S. dollar will then begin to weaken against our foreign trading partners either intentionally by our government or on its own from having too many dollars in the system from today's policies and a high budget deficit. Finally, hyperinflation has a high potential of showing up around 2020, as this is where I predict gold, which has historically been a good barometer of inflation, will reach an all-time high.

Plan accordingly and profit during these storms! Good luck!

About the Author

D aniel S. Shaffer is president and CEO of Shaffer Asset Management, Inc. He is a certified public accountant (CPA) as well as chartered financial consultant (ChFC). He has a master's of science degree in accounting from New York University and bachelor's degree in speech communications from Syracuse University.

In January of 1983, Daniel S. Shaffer started his career as a floor trader for his own account on the New York Futures Exchange. From 1983 through 1989, he was with such firms as Bear Stearns, Coopers & Lybrand (now known as PricewaterhouseCoopers), and Hambrecht & Quist (now owned by JPMorganChase). In 1989, Shaffer became an independent financial planner and money manager. He has been in the securities industry since 1983. In 2000, he developed money management strategies where he has since managed money utilizing stocks, futures, and foreign exchange for individuals, major institutions, and for his former hedge fund. In May of 2000, Shaffer joined Berthel Fisher & Company Financial Services, Inc., as a registered representative to assist individuals and business organizations attain their financial management goals.

In June of 2000, under Shaffer Asset Management, Inc.'s separate capacity as a registered investment adviser, Shaffer developed and introduced the Shaffer Stock Investment Program as an alternative investment to his predicted future of a more challenging stock market, which invests in cash, stocks, and exchange-traded funds (ETFs).

Shaffer's technical analysis of the stock, currency, and commodity futures markets has been widely recognized by the financial community and the media. He believes in helping others attain their financial goals by sharing his wealth of knowledge, research, investment experiences, and technical analysis. Shaffer Asset Management, Inc., publishes a twice-weekly newsletter called the *Shaffer Market Report*, where Shaffer outlines his opinions of multiple markets using technical analysis.

Daniel S. Shaffer is a frequently invited guest lecturer, panel member and workshop/seminar presenter for many Private Organizations and Public Events; and is often a guest commentator on national business television networks, radio shows and is quoted in the press. He is currently a featured commentator on Thestreet.com and can be found in the RealMoney section and is a contributor to www.FinanceBanter.com.

Index